Paul Theroux

ALSO BY PAUL TSONGAS

The Road From Here

*This is a Borzoi Book
published in New York
by Alfred A. Knopf*

Heading
Home

Heading Home

by Paul Tsongas

Alfred A. Knopf   New York 1984

THIS IS A BORZOI BOOK
PUBLISHED BY ALFRED A. KNOPF, INC.

Library of Congress Cataloging in Publication Data
Tsongas, Paul.   Heading home.
1. Tsongas, Paul. 2. Legislators—United States—
Biography. 3. United States. Congress. Senate—
Biography. 4. Lymphomas—Patients—United States
—Biography. I. Title.
E840.8.T77A35   1984   362.1'9699'442 [B]   84-48464
ISBN 0-394-54130-8

Manufactured in the United States of America
FIRST EDITION

Foreword

In May 1984, I was leaving a hardware store in Washington, just having purchased some rope to use in our move back to Massachusetts. I had my two-year-old daughter, Molly, in tow.

A motorcyclist pulled up next to me as we walked along the sidewalk and took off his helmet.

"She's better," he said, smiling.

"Excuse me?"

"She's better," he said, "she's better than a Senate seat." He then put on his helmet, revved up the motorcycle, and roared off.

I was warmed by this anonymous affirmation of what had occurred during the previous eight months of my life. I had gone from wanting to influence our country's present and future to just wanting to live in it and to be a full part of my family.

This book details those months. It is an attempt to describe the dilemma of setting one's priorities in our modern age.

What does it mean to step back and see your life through the prism of a diagnosis of cancer? What does it mean to possess political power, yet be hobbled by the burden of knowing that your family is being short-changed along the way?

What I went through in late 1983 and early 1984 is unique to me, but unique only in the sense of a particular set of circumstances. From the letters I've received, I know that my experiences parallel those of a great number of men and women who have had to reexamine their lives and consequently make decisions about their priorities. I hope my narrative will help them in that process.

Having decided to write this book, I went to my agent, Esther Newberg, and my editor, Ashbel Green, who were so delightful to work with when I wrote *The Road From Here: Liberalism and Realities in the 1980s* four years ago. Again they were professional, competent, and personally supportive.

I wish also to acknowledge the help on the manuscript of Marsha McMullin Ponte and Linda Manning. Indeed, my thanks to my entire Senate staff for their good and tireless work all these years.

Finally, to Niki and Ashley and Katina and Molly—I want to say thank you for making it so easy for me to love you.

Paul Tsongas
August 1984

Heading
Home

Chapter 1

Discovery

Thursday, September 29, 1983

I woke up earlier than Niki and went downstairs to enact the morning routine—let out the dog and two cats, turn off the outside lights, turn up the thermostat, and read the Washington *Post*.

Niki and I had lived in Washington for almost nine years; we had met in this city some sixteen years before when we were student interns—Niki for an investment banking firm and I for a congressman. Now I was a United States senator from Massachusetts and Niki was a law school student on extended leave to bring up a family.

Our paths to Washington wound through the West Indies (Peace Corps) and state politics for me, and New York City social work for her. We had become part of a fast-paced life-style that involved both great issues and mundane routines.

We are in truth an unlikely couple to have been in that position. We are very private, ill at ease in the world of political backslapping, and quite unwilling to devote ourselves to the social demands of Senate life. In nine years we had never given a Washington dinner party, and eventually we were dropped from the invitation lists of official Washington. But the issues side of our life—the power side, if you will—was something we thrived on.

I had competed in six elections, from the Lowell City Council to the U.S. Senate—and won them all. While even my best friends would admit that I was not a natural politician ("too low-key"), the fact remained that each political campaign had been successful. Would there be a next step up the political ladder?

I had thought about national office, but I was increasingly aware that a low-key personality did not mesh with such an undertaking. If I never went beyond the Senate, I would be grateful that I got there in the first place.

Just as I started reading the *Post*, Molly, our two-year-old, began wailing in her crib, and I went upstairs. Niki had already arrived, and the clamor had awakened Ashley and Katina. Ashley was nine and very much into reading. Katina was six and beginning first grade. All three children were quite different, and we felt ourselves blessed. The morning routine continued: the search for socks, the fight over who would get the last bagel, "No, you cannot turn on the TV," etc.

As Niki presided over the bedlam, I went to shower and shave. My mind was on next year's reelection campaign. Potential opponents kept popping up, and while the polls were very good, you never take any election lightly. I learned that lesson in 1971 when I was almost defeated for reelection to the Lowell City Council.

One name had resurfaced the day before, and I focused on his chances and how I would run against him. If he never got close in the polls, I would have to go after him—and I was weighing the various courses available. All in all, however, I didn't believe he was a serious threat.

The shower was refreshing, and my mind wandered to other matters.

It was then that I felt the lump in my groin. No pain. No discomfort. Just a lump.

"Damn."

The last thing I needed at this point was a hernia. I had become a runner in the mid-1960s and had been much more serious about it since 1977. The 1983 Boston Marathon was a goal I had trained for, only to be sidelined by an ankle injury. A hernia would kill any hopes for the 1984 marathon.

My brother-in-law had recently been operated on for a double hernia and had been out of commission for several weeks.

First, the ankle. Now, a hernia. Maybe at age forty-two I was fooling myself about running a marathon—and I'd be forty-three by then.

I got out of the shower, shaved, dressed, and went downstairs. I told Niki about the hernia on the way out of the house, walking Ashley and Katina to school. I was in a foul mood. It's not fair, I thought. Thousands upon thousands of runners never have aches, pains, or injuries. With me, it's just the opposite. How would I acquire a hernia with all my exercising and running and swimming? It didn't make any sense. I hardly noticed my two daughters beside me. I returned home, got in the car, and drove to the Capitol.

At the office I looked at my schedule for a time when I could have a hernia operation and be housebound for a couple of weeks. There was no such time. Between campaign appearances, normal Senate commitments, and speaking requests, the schedule for October and November was full. I would have to cancel a whole mess of events. It would be very inconvenient (and very expensive, since several of the speaking events had honoraria attached, and we depended on that outside income to keep our houses in Washington and Massachusetts).

In midmorning I walked across the Capitol with my foreign affairs adviser, Chris Chamberlin. The nuclear-freeze forces in the House of Representatives had scheduled a hearing on the Euromissile issue with former German chancellor Willy Brandt. Chris was also a runner, and we often went five or six miles together at noontime. As we walked to the Rayburn House Office Building, I told him about my hernia and said I would see the Capitol physician, Admiral Freeman Cary, as soon as I could.

We arrived at the hearing room, and I joined my House colleagues, including the chairman of the event, Edward Markey of Massachusetts, at the dais.

Brandt began a long presentation, urging a more rational American position on arms control. He looked a lot older and thinner than I had expected. He has a certain presence about him, a European air of intellectualism and elegance that forces you to be interested in what he says. I wondered how someone like him would fare in American politics.

I had long been involved with arms–control matters and cared passionately about these issues. Yet as Brandt read from the prepared text, my mind was flitting back and forth between Euromissiles and my hernia—and the hernia was winning. I wanted to know how bad it was and what kind of operation would be necessary.

I leaned over and asked Markey for the first crack at asking questions so I could leave. Brandt finished, and I offered some perfunctory and forgettable inquiries, which he politely answered.

At Cary's office I told the attendant I wanted to see the doctor about a hernia. Almost immediately I was ushered into his office, which was filled with pictures and mementos of his career and travels. Admiral Cary is tall, soft-spoken, and genuine. When he stands in the back of the Senate chamber on occasion, he seems bemused by the goings-on in front of him, almost like a benevolent uncle watching the play of children he is very fond of. I had never got a hint as to his political views. We chatted for a while about little things, and then I undressed and climbed up on the examining table. He felt the lump and began asking questions. He then examined me all over and raised matters that seemed unrelated to my hernia.

Finally, he said he did not know what the lump was, but it was not a hernia.

Good, I thought, no operation, and thus no interruption in my running regimen. I had been unduly alarmed.

"What do you think it is?"

"I don't know," he said. "We'll have to do some tests." He took a blood sample and an ear culture, since one ear was a bit swollen. He then began feeling around my neck and abdomen and armpits.

"It could be almost anything," he said, "but I want to find out as soon as we can." He talked about various infections and asked me if there were any cats in our house. Another member of Congress had experienced a similar problem, and it had turned out to be an infection spread by his cat. We had a cat and a new kitten, and I thought it possible I had picked up an infection. I had driven the animals from Lowell to Washington earlier that month, and the kitten had often slept on my lap. He had, in fact, urinated during the trip, and the urine had soaked into my clothes.

As we discussed this and other infection possibilities, I realized that his tone of voice and his demeanor with the staff were different from my previous visits. The easygoing amiability was missing. He was all business.

It was then that I began to understand that we might be dealing with something else. My heart skipped a beat, and I felt a surge of fear.

Lumps. Lumps. Lumps were what other people found on themselves. It couldn't be connected to me, since the physical danger I would face someday would have to do with my heart. That's why I didn't smoke and didn't drink and took exercise so seriously. My father had died of a heart attack, and that was the problem I had programmed myself to deal with. Lumps were not on the agenda. But there was one in my groin, and it was not a hernia.

Gathering up my courage, I asked him, "Well, what is the range of things we might be dealing with?" The question was cool and detached. My voice was not. It was higher than I wanted it to be.

Dr. Cary responded in the manner of a friendly, yet contained Navy physician. He went into a discussion that included lymph nodes and Hodgkin's disease. I nodded knowingly. What the hell was Hodgkin's disease? I had heard of it, of course, but I couldn't remember what it was, and I did not want to ask.

Had I experienced fever or chills recently? No, I had not. How was my appetite? All too good, thank you.

When he was finished, I dressed and he said he would call me as soon as the tests on the various infection possibilities came back. "Perhaps this afternoon."

I walked out of the Capitol to my office in the Russell Building. I didn't know what to think. I had no experience at this. The September day was bright, and the outdoors seemed to dispel the concerns I had felt in Dr. Cary's office. By the time I entered the Russell Building, I was thinking again about the campaign. The infection was not in my groin or in my office, but back with Cary. It was his responsibility now.

The day proceeded in typical fashion with appointments, meetings, and roll-call votes. We are elected to vote, but the act is often exasperating. Increasingly votes are demanded by conservative or liberal senators for the sole purpose of putting their ideological opposites on the record on difficult issues. Conservatives make liberals vote on abortion, busing, gun control, and Cuba, while liberals make conservatives vote on budget cuts in education, veterans' benefits, and social security.

After one vote in the afternoon I returned to my office, where Marsha Ponte, my secretary of seven years' standing, said Dr. Cary had called.

Cary told me that the blood tests were negative. The easiest answers to explain the lump were not the right ones. It would take a couple of days to test for more complicated items such as cat scratch, and he would ring back on Monday.

I thanked him, hung up, and felt the return of my original fear.

What could it be? Certainly nothing to be afraid of, but . . .

I phoned Niki and told her everything. We agreed that cat scratch was the only logical answer.

I still could not shift gears to worry about anything but an eventual heart problem. Years of careful behavior and exercise were my insurance, my passport to many productive decades. All this was some kind of mistake. Yet, that night, I did not sleep well.

Friday, September 30, 1983

The lump was still there when I showered the next day. What did that mean? Nothing. It was just there. It began to preoccupy me. Niki sensed my concern, and we talked about it. But what was there to say? There was a lump of unknown origins in my groin, and it was not a simple infection. We decided just to reaffirm our feelings for each other in lieu of any medical diagnosis.

Soon afterward, I was on a plane to Detroit, where I was to speak to a meeting of corporate economists. As one of the so-called neoliberals in the Democratic Party, I was often invited to talk to business groups about industrial policy and other matters involving economic development. We were arguing for a party that embraced liberal social values and yet had a concern for economic growth. Two years before I had published a book, *The Road From Here*, arguing for a policy of genuine concern for economic development and a rejection of the antibusiness sentiment that most liberals came equipped with. The book had been reasonably well received as the first treatise on this approach to Democratic politics. It had certainly resulted in a lot of speaking requests, with their own intellectual and political—and financial—advantages.

On the plane I had to go over my notes and put together the speech, but I found it impossible to concentrate. The medical tests recurred in my mind, and the speech notes never got organized.

Soon I was before the audience in a state of mental disarray. I ended up relying upon some standard jokes and an old but tested speech to get through the event.

Talking to an audience was not enough to fill the void in my stomach. Even during the question-and-answer period, my concentration drifted. For the first of many times I would operate on two levels—going through the motions of a normal life with a mind totally absorbed with what was going on in my body.

It was clear that it was going to be a long time until Monday. By midafternoon, I was back in my office trying to behave normally—and not doing very well. Dennis Kanin came in to discuss an issue. He had been my chief aide, campaign manager, neighbor, and close friend since the 1974 Congressional campaign. Our wives had briefly managed a dessert business together. I told him what was happening; there was no point in pretending with him.

I used the words "Hodgkin's disease" with a curious sense of detachment. The words were there, the fear was there, but there was no sense that it would be the eventual answer. Dennis told me about a former co-worker of his who had had Hodgkin's disease several years ago and had gone through weeks of agonizing chemotherapy, but was now fine as far as he knew. I didn't know how to react to that.

With an increasing sense of ignorance, I decided to tap the resources of the Boston medical community for some expert advice. But the only person I really knew well was Dr. Mary Ellen Avery of Boston's Children's Hospital. She referred me to a Dr. George Canellos at the Dana-Farber Cancer Institute. I called him, but he was out of the country, so I spoke to his assistant, Dr. Skarin, who was upbeat about Hodgkin's disease, saying we had learned a great deal about it. The institute would be glad to consult.

The weekend dragged by. I had an odd time with Ashley and Katina and Molly. I was worried about the unknown but didn't even know how to worry about it. Should I go about my normal routine? Should I banish concern from my thoughts or begin the process of accepting a new reality? And exactly how could I do that with a nine-, six-, and two-year-old as weekend companions?

Niki was less hampered by my seemingly endless weighing of options. She went to the public library on Connecticut Avenue to read up on Hodgkin's disease. I did not want to read about it. I did not want to talk about it. It was the sole subject on my mind, but it was sealed in my lips.

Monday, October 3, 1983

On Monday I was scheduled to speak to a national convention of auto-parts dealers in Boston. The trip to the airport was reminiscent of the Friday before—a sense of dislocation. The Detroit speech experience had been unsettling, and now I had to do it again. I did not look forward to another session with Dr. Cary, but the idea of going through a normal routine far away from the support of my family was even more cheerless. I was becoming aware of how much my strength in difficult circumstances was a function of what surrounded me.

The plane, however, was delayed in Washington, and I sat and waited. If the delay was long enough, I realized, I could legitimately call off my appearance in Boston. But people were expecting me, and I should go through with it. I was not going to begin putting my life on hold.

I decided to let circumstances decide. If I could get to Boston in time to speak, I'd go. If there turned out to be only enough time for a rushed five-minute routine, I'd skip it. The delay continued, and I left the terminal.

Returning to the parking lot to retrieve my car, I felt both relieved and guilty, but mostly relieved. The lump was the issue. Other things would just have to wait.

Office affairs were impossible to deal with, so I went to the

Senate gym on the first floor of the Russell Building. By modern health-club standards, the gym is antiquated, but it has a good staff, a small pool, a sauna, a steam room, and a variety of equipment. I threw myself into a workout with a kind of manic vigor—trying to exercise away my fears and to prove to myself that the old body could still bench-press and swim and do sit-ups. The capacity to perform adequately was reassuring. I felt strong, so I felt good. Having accomplished all the possible exercises, there was no choice but to return to the office.

Walking through the corridors, I realized how much this painless, omnipresent lump was affecting my capacity to cope— and I didn't know what to do about it.

I had been in many positions of stress and in many strange places around the world. In the early 1960s I had lived in Ethiopia as a Peace Corps volunteer and had had no fears whatever. As a member of Congress, I had traveled to foreign countries where there was the possibility of physical danger, but I had always been confident about my ability to deal with the unexpected. Now I was drifting, and I did not like what I saw in myself. Events were controlling me, not vice versa. It was not what I had ever expected to experience.

The afternoon wore on without a word from Dr. Cary. I had no intention of making the first call.

While I was in a meeting with a group of constituents, Marsha Ponte stuck her head in the door to say that Dr. Cary was on the phone. My heart leaped. Picking up the phone in my office with all those people present was impractical. "Tell him I'll call back," I said, and no sooner were the words out of my mouth than I grabbed the phone and said hello. Waiting any longer was impossible.

"I just wanted to tell you that we have the results of the ear culture and you do have an ear infection. When I see you later, I'll give you some drops to put in it," Dr. Cary said.

"Oh, okay," I responded. Silence.

"The blood tests related to the lump are not back yet. I'll call you when they are," he said.

"Thank you," I said weakly.

My head was spinning. An ear infection. A goddam ear infection. I didn't want to hear about an ear infection—what the hell was that lump in my groin? What were those lab people doing, anyway? Didn't they realize how critical all this was? Needless to say, the remainder of the meeting and the remainder of the day were unproductive.

I told Dennis Kanin of the developing situation, and he was again very sympathetic, but since his wife, Carol, had delivered a baby two weeks before, there was a clear limit to his focus.

There was no further call from Dr. Cary, so I went home. Niki listened to my account of his call, and we again reviewed the various possibilities. She was very clear-headed about it all. As a young girl, Niki was an athlete as well as a top student. Her best sport was diving, and she had great promise. One day when she was twelve, she received a jolt, and the retina in her eye detached. She spent long weeks immobile in the hospital after her eye operations.

That terminated her athletic career. Any activity that could jar her was prohibited—running, tennis, horseback riding, and diving. Her exercise would be limited to fluid motions that did not carry the threat of abrupt jolts. She was thus aware of physical limits and the vulnerability of the body.

I had never experienced illness or serious injury. I earned a swimming letter at Dartmouth, played soccer in Ethiopia, and took up running during law school. I had known goals, not limits.

Eventually we exhausted the issue. We could not sit around and discuss endlessly something we knew so little about. We decided to get a baby-sitter and go to a movie. The film was a French farce called *Pauline at the Beach* which involved various personal liaisons and such. It was supposed to be funny and had received some good reviews. I found it intolerably mindless, and we left halfway through. I was not in the mood to watch an endless series of casual encounters.

It was difficult to sleep that night. Whatever was going on physically, I clearly had a lot to learn about dealing with this kind of stress. In contrast, Niki was very optimistic. She was better informed, having read all she could about what I might have. She knew the boundaries that were out there.

Tuesday, October 4, 1983

The day dragged on. No call from Dr. Cary until the afternoon. He informed me that all the tests had come back negative, but he wanted to see me right away.

All the tests were negative! They hadn't found an answer.

No cat scratch. Then what was it? Well, it wasn't going to be an easy answer.

I told Niki the news. As usual, she was much more positive than I was. "Don't jump to conclusions. Go see Dr. Cary and find out what's what."

Leaving the office, I informed Marsha as casually as I could where I was going. She looked at me quizzically. This was unusual behavior, and any more of it would start the office rumor mill.

On the way to Cary's office, I was again upset at my lack of composure. I had been thrown off stride, and my internal resources were clearly inadequate. I needed time to adjust, to reprogram my concerns, to contemplate and assimilate an entirely new set of medical realities. But there was no time. The lump had entered my life only five days ago. I would have to do better—and fast.

Dr. Cary examined me all over again. He then took me across the hall for an x-ray. In the darkened room with my chest against the cold plate of the x-ray machine, I felt the dread. And for the first time, I turned to a higher authority. "Please, God." I whispered loud enough for Him to hear, but no one else.

Cary studied the x-rays with another physician. They talked quietly and clinically—I didn't know whether to listen. I could only hear parts of the conversation, so I tuned it all out. Then the other doctor examined me as well.

He felt my neck, my armpits, my groin, my stomach, my abdomen. He asked questions.

"I want you to be seen by a specialist," Dr. Cary said finally. He called Bethesda Naval Hospital and made an appointment the next day with a Dr. Shen. I didn't ask who Dr. Shen was, but Cary made it clear that Hodgkin's was the focus of attention.

Meanwhile my ear infection was checked again by an eye-ear-nose-and-throat specialist. The exam was not limited to my ear. Discussing the lump, he dismissed any real concern. The chances were overwhelming, he said, that it was a normal infection and the lymph nodes had just swollen.

As he went on describing his own specialty and cases he'd seen of unexplained lumps and bumps, I feasted on his reassurance. He was a specialist; he must know what he was talking about. In fact, he said, if he were in my shoes he wouldn't even go to Bethesda, he'd just observe it for a few days and see what happened. Sounded reasonable to me. I turned around to face Dr. Cary, and one look at his expression was all I needed. He was visibly annoyed at the other doctor. Cary was responsible for the health of senators, and he took his responsibility very seriously. For him, no margin of possible error was acceptable. His voice was stern and bordered on the rude. I could feel the admiral in him take over. I was going to Bethesda and that was that. It was the only time I ever saw him display anger.

I desperately wanted to go home and talk with Niki and see the children. But I had committed myself to speak at the American Business Conference. I had been very active with Dr. George Hatsopoulos, president of ThermoElectron, a high-tech firm in Waltham, Massachusetts, who had done an important study of the cost of capital in the United States and Japan. The situation had enormous implications for the future of high technology, a matter of great interest to me, and for the economy of both Massachusetts and the country. The American Business Conference had cosponsored his study, and this was a unique opportunity to address its membership. One hundred and twenty-five chief executive officers of high-growth companies—a chance to offer my view of economic growth and to prove to a mostly Republican audience that not all Democrats are antibusiness, that there are liberals who don't regard "profit" as a dirty word.

The event was held in the Cannon Caucus Room, a magnificent chamber on the House side of the Capitol. The dinner and small talk were hard to endure. The time with Dr. Cary was real, the cost of capital irrelevant. But when I got up to speak, my mind was all business. The issue of an aggressive industrial strategy was important to me, and I had devoted a great deal of time to trying to force a public debate on it. I talked without distraction, answered questions, and finished to warm applause. It was like normal times. Only when I sat down did the next day's meeting with Dr. Shen reenter my consciousness. No, it was not like normal times. There was another agenda.

After the dinner, I was invited to have drinks with some of the participants. My standard excuse that I had to get home and see my family was accepted without comment.

Niki and I had spoken on the phone after the session with Cary, so she knew what had transpired. When I told her about the appointment with Shen, she asked whether I expected her to be there as well. "Well, I don't think so. I'll let you know what he says," I answered.

That was a mistake.

Niki is a very calm, even-tempered person, but this was too much. She rebuked me for wanting to cope with the situation on my own, for excluding her when she was to be affected as well, and for trying to be some sort of old-world macho figure, braving it "like a man." Was I embarrassed to bring along my wife? Would the doctors see that as a sign of weakness on my part? She was furious.

I was taken aback.

Here I was seeking warm sympathy and instead I was being labeled an insensitive fool. I was outraged, but it was no use. Niki was right, and I finally agreed with her. As the commercial goes, "I needed that."

That was when I realized the difference between a sympathetic ear and a partner in distress. If I wanted to crawl into a hole of self-pity, she would not keep me company. She would drag me out as unceremoniously as necessary. She was going to be a drill sergeant if I didn't straighten myself out. She then proceeded to tell me what she had learned that day about Hodgkin's disease, and I listened.

It was a reversal of roles. I was the resident expert on heart-related matters. Hodgkin's disease was her domain. But even more, she was now the rock. Our life together had pretty much flowed according to my career needs. Niki had given up law school to raise our family. It had been a difficult decision, but she had come to accept it and live with it. Inevitably, however, it meant that I defined who we were to the outside world. I was the successful combatant of those six campaigns, I held the press conferences to speak out on issues, I got pieces of legislation passed and appeared on television.

Niki did her job well, but our society doesn't really celebrate a parent who rears children with devotion. Smith College and Boston University Law School had been succeeded by menus and diapers and parent-teacher conferences. She was confident of the value of all this, but the larger world wasn't. "And what do you do?" she was often asked in career-oriented Washington. "I'm raising our children." "Oh," would come the embarrassed reply, and the subject would quickly be changed.

Somehow I had grown to accept the routine. But the new situation called for a different strength.

My supply was deficient.

Niki's wasn't.

Wednesday, October 5, 1983

The next morning I flew to Boston to receive the Massachusetts AFL-CIO endorsement at the Park Plaza Hotel. At the convention site, I went around shaking hands from table to table. Again my consciousness was on two tracks. When the session began, I was introduced by Arthur Osborne, the state council president and a strong supporter. This was a very important event for me, because organized labor had always looked askance at my "neo-liberalism." They were more in tune with Tip O'Neill and Ted Kennedy; my style was different—too "Republican," a union leader once said, despite a solid pro-labor voting record.

My speech was an attack on President Reagan's economic program—particularly the deficits. I spoke as forcefully as I could and pounded the lectern a few times. On a scale of ten, it was a three at best. No standing ovation like that from the businessmen the night before. Just a typically polite response. Businessmen expect liberal Democrats to be ogres. When you come across as reasonably thoughtful, they are delighted. But labor audiences anticipate speeches that reflect your complete commitment to their cause, and anything less leaves them flat.

In spite of all this, I got their unanimous endorsement, but I knew my speech would not linger in their minds. On the plane to Washington, I brooded about why it was I couldn't turn on such an audience when I could easily rouse college students or businessmen or a foreign-policy seminar. Perhaps my approach was too cerebral—the capacity to excite a labor meeting required a different skill, one I would have to develop if I wanted to go anywhere beyond the Senate. It was comfortable to focus again on political ambitions.

Anyway, I was pleased by the endorsement and my close relationship with the union hierarchy. Any primary opponent would have a difficult time if he chose to run. Any Democrat taking me on had to sew up particular constituencies that were angry at me for various reasons—labor because of my support for a wage freeze on the Chrysler bail-out legislation, the Jewish community because of my criticism of the Israeli bombing of Beirut. I had pretty much restored my relationship with both groups, and the labor endorsement was symbolic of that rapprochement.

The closer the plane got to Washington, the more these political considerations gave way to concern about the Bethesda appointment.

At the Senate I filmed a public-television debate on Nicaragua, arguing the "liberal" perspective against Charles Krauthammer of *The New Republic*. Although my Third World interests had always centered on Africa, events had compelled me to be quite involved in our policies involving both El Salvador and Nicaragua. The debate was intense, and again I found myself totally immersed in the subject. I left the studio feeling pleased with myself.

I picked up Niki at home, and we drove out Wisconsin Avenue to the Bethesda Naval Hospital. We found a parking place in the Bethesda garage after much driving around. We also had difficulty at the front desk trying to find out where we were supposed to go. Finally, we found ourselves at the Oncology Department. "Oncology"—the word had never registered in my mind before.

It was a word I would have to get used to.

Another word I was not accustomed to was "cancer." Six days after I had found the lump, the word had not yet entered conversation. "Hodgkin's disease," "lymph nodes," "oncology"—I heard them all over and over, but not "cancer." The Oncology Department brought the word closer. The room was filled with people who were being examined for or treated for cancer.

I felt totally alien. I was one of the select few in the United States Senate—the most exclusive club in the world. I did not want membership in a club of the afflicted.

Niki and I made small talk. I was very happy she was there. I had this irrelevant flashback about walking through the ladies' underwear department at Woodward & Lothrop on the way to the children's section. Because Niki was with me, my being there was acceptable. She was like a guide whose mere presence signaled that everything was all right.

Dr. Shen was a young resident, shy but obviously very intelligent. He took me to see Dr. Charles Veach, the head of the Oncology Department. Veach was a handsome, reserved, soft-spoken man who chose his words carefully.

After a short discussion, we went into another room and both Shen and Veach examined me. They told me there were swollen lymph nodes in my neck and my armpits. Veach also showed me my chest x-rays and the areas of concern there.

My sense of seriousness escalated dramatically. It was not just one lump. They were all over the place. All through my damn body.

Back in Veach's office, the doctors talked to Niki and me about Hodgkin's disease and the various other possibilities. We discussed percentages of cure. We went into great length about treatment.

If it was Hodgkin's disease, the usual treatment would be intense chemotherapy in a determined bid to wipe it out. No one speculated about what would happen if this process failed. There were procedures and there were statistical odds, and I would have to toss the dice.

I tried to react normally and ask the expected questions. Niki was more aggressive. Armed with the information she had accumulated, she was able to ask the proper clinical questions and get detailed answers. I was being fatalistic; she was being combative. I remember looking over at this beautiful mother of my three children and thinking, Boy, are you strong.

Dr. Veach said he wanted to perform a biopsy as soon as possible, by removing either the lymph node in my groin or the one in my neck. Before I could respond, Niki agreed. She had been told by a doctor friend that I should have had a biopsy right when the lump was discovered.

Friday was the first available time. They could do it the next day, but it would mean canceling out some other patient.

He looked at me for direction. I assumed he was offering me the decision. Because I was a senator I could insist on going to the head of the line. It was clear that Veach was reluctant to indulge that kind of privilege, and so was I. "Friday is fine," I said.

Niki drove me back to the office, where I canceled a dinner commitment with Frank Conroy, a writer friend who works for the National Endowment for the Arts. I could not go through much more pretense, nor could I begin to confide in other people.

I spent the evening quietly at home.

Thursday, October 6, 1983

Thursday morning I opened the office drawer that contained all my personal financial records and began to calculate my net worth, my life insurance, and what financial shape I would leave Niki and the girls in if things went wrong.

I asked Marsha to call the Andover Savings Bank. I wanted to find out whether I had life insurance on the first mortgage of our house in Lowell.

I did—about $55,000 worth.

I then phoned the Senate office that handles life insurance. Life insurance had always seemed to me an excessive drain on a limited salary. On January 13, 1981, however, my attitude had changed.

On that date, during a snowstorm, an Air Florida plane crashed into the 14th Street Bridge and then into the Potomac River. All but six of the seventy-four people aboard the plane were killed. It took days to recover all the bodies.

I was aboard the plane that took off immediately before the Air Florida flight. Every time I passed the crash site on the way from Alexandria (where we then lived) to Washington and saw the work crews trying to fish out the aircraft and bodies, I shuddered. As a result, I took out the maximum life insurance available under the Senate plan.

Yes, the disbursing office said, I was fully covered.

I absorbed the information and calculated how far it would go. It was all I would ever be able to get. No one was going to give me more life insurance now.

The numbers made it clear that Niki could not afford to continue living in Washington. The mortgage payments were just too high. She would have to sell the Washington house and return to Lowell. I felt bad that she would not have an option. What would she want to do? Would she be happy in Lowell if I wasn't there with her? What about finishing law school? It would be very tight.

I spent the entire morning figuring out every last detail. The whole effort gave me an enormous sense of purpose. On balance, the situation wasn't great, but it wasn't disastrous either. It was ironic that the Air Florida crash had put my family in a better position because of my life-insurance decision. Had it not been for that tragedy, our potential financial situation would have been much more precarious. Finally, I decided not to think about it anymore.

Later that day Marsha told me that a Dr. Veach had confirmed the appointment at Bethesda the next morning at 8:30 a.m. I was to ask for a Dr. Ghosh when I got there.

"Thanks," I said.

She looked at me. She and my executive assistant, Chris Naylor, worked in the room just outside my office, and both had been with me all through my Senate years. We were all very close. She obviously realized by now that something was wrong and wanted to know what it was.

I got up and said I was going to the gym. Thank God for the

gym! I was in no mood to talk about this other half of my life being played out at Bethesda. Dennis Kanin and my chief legislative aide, Rich Arenberg, knew, and that was all. Dennis, Rich, and I had been together since the 1974 campaign for Congress and had made all the political decisions together. I felt guilty about excluding others, but I wanted to keep it to myself.

That night turned out rather oddly. There was a $500-a-person fundraiser being given me at the office of Tom Boggs, a well-known Washington lawyer and lobbyist, cohosted by Bob Berry, a friend and lobbyist for General Electric. It was designed to pull in Washington money for the campaign. My expected Republican opponent, Ray Shamie, was 55 percentage points behind in the polls. He had lost to Ted Kennedy in the 1982 campaign by 22 points and was going to take me on now, but he would get little support from the business community in Massachusetts. Given all this, the fundraiser should have been a success.

The Senate was in session, so I had to take my chances on being across the city on 25th Street where Boggs's office was located. It was the same building where Walter Mondale worked, a new brick complex with a marvelous view of Georgetown. I reached Boggs's office around 6:45 p.m. He was there. Five or six others were there. And that was it. We were about sixty people short. Where was everyone? "It's still early," I was told.

Just as Niki arrived, my beeper went off, signaling a vote in the Senate. I ran out the door, raced against the traffic back to the Capitol, and barely made the vote. On the return drive I was hoping that the crowds would have arrived, but it was not to be.

The attendance had swollen by a grand total of eight more people. I looked at my watch; it was 7:25, and the reception was billed from 6:30 to 8:30. My experience told me that after the first hour as many people would leave as would arrive. This would be the peak attendance.

Everyone felt very awkward. "There are a lot of other fund-raisers this evening." "It's too early to raise money since the campaign is so quiet." "Maybe people are still on the Hill, since the Senate is still in session." But the event was a failure, and all the small talk was not going to change that.

Around 8:30 a small group gathered around Tom Boggs, who was blunt. "You're the problem, Senator. People don't know you. We called a lot of people, and most of them said they had never met you. You're on the wrong Senate committees to raise money from, and you compound the problem by never trying to meet people."

Tom Boggs is not accustomed to fundraisers that bomb, and he was not pleased.

His candor was uncharacteristic for Washington. You don't confront a senator with harsh reality, no matter how glaring it may be. But Boggs let me have it without a trace of hostility or disrespect. It was just cold analysis delivered by a pro.

He was absolutely right.

And I didn't give a damn.

I had heard this criticism before—especially from my chief fundraiser, Nick Rizzo, of Andover, Massachusetts, not to mention others who tried to raise money in D.C. Niki and I did not frequent the social circuit, and we knew it cost us. But the kids were more important to us than being regulars on Embassy Row or in hotel ballrooms. Senate duties wreaked havoc with my weekends. I was constantly absent, and it was difficult for all of us. If I went out weekday evenings on the Washington whirl, the children would be almost totally fatherless.

And in twelve hours I would be in Bethesda Hospital having a lymph node removed to see whether it was malignant. In that context, what difference did it make if the representatives of various companies and associations had never met me?

I had contemplated the trade-offs and opted for home. And I made no apologies for it. I told Boggs that his analysis was correct, that I had known it for a long time and had accepted it. He was not placated.

Niki and I left before the guests. We had arrived in separate cars and drove home separately. She took Chris Naylor's daughter, Laura, our baby-sitter, home, and I waited for her to return. I don't think we've ever been closer than we were then.

The fundraiser bust had been a source of strange delight. The event flopped in part because we had invested our time in each other and in Ashley, Katina, and Molly. It was as if this failure in one sector of our lives emphasized our success in the other. We had made the right choices; and if people thought us unsocial, so be it. Our children loved us, and in this crisis it was the family unit that counted. Official Washington would do very well without our social presence.

Friday, October 7, 1983

The next morning Niki and I met with the surgical team, Dr. Ghosh and Dr. Fletcher. Ghosh had come originally from Pakistan, and Fletcher from Massachusetts.

As we waited in the reception room, I handed Niki a folder with a complete financial statement, what the options were, how to sell the Washington house, etc. I told her to read it while the biopsy was taking place. I wasn't being morbid or pessimistic— I just wanted her to read it. During these eight days, Niki had not allowed discussion of what might happen. But she had to know these financial details. In the context of the surgery, the topic seemed for some odd reason to be less objectionable.

The operating room was cold, and I felt strange lying on the table. Could this really be happening to me? I hadn't been in an operating room since the removal of my tonsils more than three decades ago. Yet here I was, and here the doctors were. They decided to go into the groin area, since the other lymph nodes were too small. They prepared me and began the procedure.

"Are you a Democrat or Republican?" one of the nurses asked.

"A Democrat."

"I know a very nice Republican—from Nevada, I think. He's a senator."

"Is it Paul Laxalt?"

"Yes, that's his name. He's really very nice."

"He's one of the decent people in politics."

"Don't you have to be a nice guy to be successful in politics?"

I laughed. They were trying to distract me with conversation, and it was working. I explained how many s.o.b.s there were in my business. It was unlike medicine, I said, because in medicine it doesn't make any difference whether you are perceived as nice or not. Needless to say, that precipitated a lively give-and-take. Meanwhile the surgeons were tugging and pulling and probing, trying to remove the lymph node. I could not see anything, since a tentlike arrangement had been set up to prevent me from breathing onto the surgical area.

Finally, the lymph node was located and extracted. I couldn't see what it looked like. I thought about asking to have it shown to me. Maybe people were queasy about seeing their innards. What would I be looking for? Nothing in particular. I was then sewn up, the lymph node was placed in solution, and Dr. Shen came to get it.

I dressed and slowly walked out of the room. The groin area was still numb, but there was some dull pain. I picked up Niki in the reception area, and we started slowly toward the escalator. Niki asked me when we would get the results.

"I don't know," I replied.

"You don't know? What do you mean, you don't know? Are we going to find out today or are we going to have to wait until Tuesday?" (Monday was Columbus Day and thus a holiday.) Niki was incredulous at my lack of information. Why hadn't I asked such an obvious question? I did not have a good answer.

We were called by Dr. Fletcher, pursuing us down the escalator. He said that the tests ought to give us some clues by the afternoon, but nothing definite would be known until Tuesday.

Did we want to be called with the preliminary results or wait until Tuesday when all of the results would be known?

"Tuesday will be fine," I said.

"That doesn't make sense," Niki said. "Call us today. I don't want to spend another weekend waiting."

Okay, he said, as soon as they had anything worth passing on, he would phone. Would we be available?

"I'll be available," I said. "I'm going back to the office and do some jogging." It was meant to be funny, but no one laughed.

The whole affair left me oddly euphoric. The dread had suddenly disappeared. The operation had been a positive act. We were doing something about it. I felt almost giddy. Rather than stay home, I asked Niki to drive me to the office. We were taking up the farm bill, and I wanted to vote on it. I had never felt that way about a farm bill before. Maybe I was now back in control.

By noon I was in the office and kept a luncheon appointment with Bob Baker, head of economic development in Lynn, Massachusetts. We went over to the Senate Dining Room and met with the Skigas brothers, who were setting up a high-technology plant in Lynn. We discussed business and our shared Greek background.

One of the Skigases mentioned his wife's recent death from cancer. He had no way of knowing how much I could identify with his feelings.

During the afternoon, there were roll-call votes and a lot of walking back and forth between the Senate chambers in the Capitol and my office in the Russell Building. The numbness was gone, and my groin hurt. Walking made it worse. On one vote, Chris Chamberlin came with me and noticed my slow, stiff gait. He said nothing, but I could sense his mind churning. Since walking was so painful, I decided to stay put in the Capitol. I lay down in the Marble Room, a high-ceilinged room off the Senate chambers where senators can read or nap or work. I could vote by walking only ten yards rather than making the seven-minute hike from my office.

Lying on a couch with the hectic activity of the Senate in the next room was like observing a ritual as a nonparticipant. Whenever I had stopped by that room before, it had been to read the newspapers or the *Economist* or to nap during late-night sessions.

Now I felt removed from it all. The other senators had their concerns. Mine was very different.

Periodically I phoned the office and asked Marsha whether there were any calls.

"Calls from whom?" she asked once.

"Oh, anyone."

There weren't any.

"Are you coming back to the office?"

"Yes."

"When?"

"Soon."

By now the office must have been rife with speculation. The life of a senator is totally scheduled, every weekday and almost every weekend. There are no gaps of time to do nothing in. My daily life was known to all my staff. These sudden doctor's appointments and my disappearances were unprecedented. Dennis Kanin would later tell me that staff members kept coming to him and demanding to know what was happening.

Finally the bells rang four times, signaling the end of the day's session. I remained on the couch for a few minutes, then reluctantly went back to my office. Soon after my return, Marsha told me that Dr. Veach was calling.

I had no emotion. What was, was. It had already been decided; this was just the passing of information.

The tests were just preliminary, Veach cautioned, and the full results would not be in until Tuesday, but he wanted to tell me what they knew at this point.

His words were measured. I had nodular lymphoma. "It is not . . . benign."

Chapter 2

Reality

"It is not benign."

What an interesting way of putting it. Rather than "It is malignant," it sounded better to say "It is not benign."

They mean the same thing. Yet as a patient awaiting test results, the word that reverberates around your head is "malignant," not "benign." When the first three words are "It is not," you want the following word to be "malignant."

The tests would show that the lump "is malignant" or "is not malignant." The tests could also be used to show that the lump "is benign." They would not, of course, be used to show that "it is not benign." If the news was bad, the method of conveyance would be "It is malignant."

There was no room in this exchange for the sentence "It is not benign."

Thus did my mind work. Focused on a phrase. I thought how final it was. If the sentence had been "It is not malignant," I was back to campaign thoughts and financial worries and presumptions of "I'm gonna live forever."

But he had said, "It is not benign," and as a result everything changed. A door clanged shut behind me.

I sat at my desk and wrote down the information on a yellow legal-size pad. It was all very preliminary, and we would have to wait until Tuesday for final results, but this in essence was what we were dealing with. Veach went on to describe the various possibilities of treatment. Much would depend upon whether the lymphoma was "indolent" or had become aggressive. The lymphoma was probably treatable, but not curable. I asked him to call Dr. Skarin and Dr. Canellos in Boston. He agreed.

"Thank you."

I hung up the phone and sat in silence. A new part of my life had begun. The previous chapters were behind me, and there was only the future—a future that would be different.

The favorable odds had turned out to be a delusion. It could have been a hernia. It wasn't. It could have been a simple infection. It wasn't. It could have been cat scratch. It wasn't. It could have been benign. It wasn't. It could have been malignant, yet curable, like Hodgkin's disease. It wasn't.

It made no sense at all. I took risks when I went abroad to trouble spots. I accepted the possibility of eventual heart trouble. That was the program. This was alien. Could it be that it was all a mistake? The lump was real. It had been removed, and tested. But maybe they would get different results by Tuesday. Maybe, but not likely.

I called home. Niki had errands to do and was going to be in and out. She answered the phone, and I was grateful she was there.

In a voice I thought remarkably calm, I relayed the information in clinical, detached terms. The message was medical, not human.

"Well, we're just going to beat it, that's all," she said. "Come on home."

A logistical problem. She had my car. "Wait there and I'll pick you up as soon as Ashley and Katina are out of school, in about twenty minutes." It was agreed that I would meet them at 3:30 on the street outside the Russell Building.

Dennis Kanin and Rich Arenberg came in and closed the door, and I told them the news. "It is malignant." They were absolutely lost for words. What do you say to someone in those circumstances? Dennis and Rich would be the first of hundreds of people, some of whom cared for me and some of whom did not, but all of whom would struggle to find the right thing to say.

I was in Washington and in the United States Senate, but I wasn't. My world was no longer expansive and reaching, but closed and shrinking.

The time had come to tell the family. I called my stepsister, Vicki Peters, in Lowell. Vicki was twenty-eight years old, married, the mother of two boys. She answered the phone, and I said I had something to tell her.

"I have cancer."

For the first time in nine days of this demon, I actually spoke the dreaded word. The word broke the dam, and the tears flowed. That moment marked the reality. I had cancer.

The talk was brief, and I said I'd ring back later that night. I tried to call my twin sister, Thaleia, who was a fundraiser for the Institute of Contemporary Art in Boston and a true political activist. More relevantly, she had been a nurse and had married a doctor. She would be familiar with most of this. She wasn't at her office. I left a message for her to call me at home—"It's very important."

I phoned Niki and told her I would get a ride home and enlisted Rich as my chauffeur.

I canceled appointments for Tuesday. There was no use in going through the pretense of normalcy. I had been scheduled to fly to Massachusetts for a speech to the Harvard Business Club and other such appearances. There would be no way of calling off an early-Tuesday-morning event after the holiday. It could not be helped. By now Chris and Marsha would be on full alert, but without knowing what to be alert about.

It was a sunny and marvelous day. As we drove down Constitution Avenue to Virginia Avenue to Rock Creek Park to Massachusetts Avenue to 34th Street, we passed much of the glory of Washington. I looked at all this wonder with detachment—as if I were a former resident and now living somewhere else.

Our conversation was calm and reasoned and sensible. For Rich it must have been a very long fifteen minutes. He had been with me through the campaigns and had overseen our legislative efforts. Now he had another task. There were no profound remarks to be made. Just companionship. We drove up Lowell Street onto 35th Street and came to the curb in front of the house. I thanked Rich for his friendship and his understanding and walked into the house.

Ashley and Katina were playing in the downstairs den.

"Hi, Daddy."

"Hi. Where's Mommy?"

"She's upstairs."

I went to the bedroom; Niki was on the phone with Thaleia. I took the receiver and was just as emotional as I had been with Vicki. My detachment of the drive home had vanished.

The days of waiting and wondering and fearing had ended with our hopes dashed. There was only bad news—terrible news.

That afternoon, as we sat on the bed, we felt crushed by the waves of anger and frustration and hopelessness that washed over us. All I could be thankful for was Niki and her strength and her love.

While Ashley and Katina played downstairs and Molly slept in the next room, the absorption of the reality of cancer began:

How long will I live?

I'm only forty-two years old. Molly won't even remember me.

My mind raced back to my mother, whose picture stood on the dresser. She had died from tuberculosis when she was thirty-eight and I was seven. Her illness had apparently been aggravated by my and Thaleia's birth, and by the time we were a year and a half, she had to be institutionalized.

My father moved us to live with my grandparents and aunt

in a big old house on Highland Street in Lowell. For all intents and purposes, my grandmother became my mother, and we even called her Ma. She and my grandfather were Greek immigrants who had brought over my father and his siblings when they were quite young. It was a close, ethnic, traditional, and caring family.

Emotionally this arrangement would serve me well, because I would never have contact with my mother again, and thus I did not feel her loss. Occasionally we would be taken to the sanitarium in Vermont, where we played in the yard outside the building so that she could see us from the window. Because of the fear of contagion, there was never any physical contact or meeting.

That afternoon I looked at her picture and ached about what those six years in the sanitarium must have been for her. To look out from a hospital room at your twins and know that you could not hold them and that they would never have a sense of you.

The cure for tuberculosis would not come in time. Would I suffer the same fate?

I also thought about my father. He had died two years before. But he had seen me become a United States senator, and it had filled him with great satisfaction. Yet he had buried my mother and my stepmother and one baby. He had worked hard at his business, but Lowell's economic decline had robbed him of financial success. Life had been a real struggle, but he deeply loved his children and showed it. What were the lessons of his experience?

We had our differences, of course. He was a conservative Republican who revered his fellow Greek Spiro Agnew and admired Richard Nixon. Needless to say, our political discussions were not easy ones. He had gone to Harvard and looked with disfavor at my Dartmouth and Yale Law affiliations.

We did agree on more important matters. The Red Sox. Niki (even though she wasn't Greek), Ashley, and Katina. He was a real old-world figure when it came to family.

I wished he had lived long enough to see Molly.

Now I felt relieved that he did not have to know that his son had cancer.

Molly woke up with a wail, and Niki brought her into the room. Just her presence allowed me to feel gratitude as well as loss.

When the emotions subsided, we decided to get out of the house and find a restaurant. We couldn't stay there and hash everything over and over again.

We very seldom went out for dinner except to Swenson's or McDonald's or Roy Rogers or Armand's Pizza or some such basic family place. This time would be different.

The kids got excited, and we drove out toward Maryland. We stopped for gasoline in the Spring Valley section of Washington. Nearby was the Bread Oven restaurant. It looked very quaint and just right, but it would not open until 6:00 p.m., and that was half an hour away. The kids couldn't last that long. "Daddy, I'm starving."

We continued on to Maryland, driving toward Great Falls, and found a delightful outdoor restaurant, the Old Angler's Inn. The kids were fascinated by the place with its gardens and walkways. It would be a wonderful diversion. Unfortunately I had not even thought about paying for dinner and had not brought sufficient money. The prices were listed on a menu displayed outside the door, and we only had enough for three of us to eat. (I have never carried credit cards.)

"Girls, we aren't going to eat here," I said finally.

"Oh, Daddy, I'm starving. This is very nice—why can't we stay?"

"We're not going to eat here? We left the other place and now we're going to leave this place. Daddy, what's going on?"

"Well, we are going to go somewhere else," I replied.

"Why somewhere else? We want to eat here."

"Daddy, we want to eat here. We've been driving and driving, and we're very hungry and we won't leave. Mommy, can't we eat here?"

I took Katina and Ashley aside.

"We don't have enough money," I said.

"What do you mean, we don't have enough money?"

"Well, this restaurant is more expensive than I thought it would be. So we have to go someplace else. I didn't think about bringing enough money."

They just looked at me.

We piled everyone back into the car and headed back toward Washington. The conversation now focused not on the Bread Oven or the Old Angler's Inn but on more familiar turf, McDonald's versus Swenson's.

The entire effort was one of breaking free from the gloom, to be together, to do something different and exciting. McDonald's did not qualify.

We agreed on Swenson's. Or rather, I said we were going to Swenson's and that was that. Ashley and Katina brooded in the back seat while Molly moaned about being hungry. The drive back to Washington was very long indeed.

At Swenson's on Wisconsin Avenue we ordered our food, and the kids played the Pac Man game. They bounced back and forth during the next hour, leaving Niki and me to talk quietly, to look at them with a sense that every moment should be profound.

"Don't drink all your Coke before the food comes," I said profoundly to Katina. She was not impressed by this father-daughter discourse.

I could not eat, which was not so unusual during this period, but I derived enormous pleasure from the four people who were sharing my life.

We returned home and put the children to bed. That simple act, taken for granted before and often impossible to do at all because of my schedule, was deeply moving.

After they were asleep, we called Niki's parents on Cape Cod and told them the news. "Oh, Paul," my mother-in-law said. "Oh, Paul." She and my father-in-law had four daughters, and

I had been their first son-in-law. Their anguish was that of parents, not in-laws.

It was a long, long night—and we woke up a good while before first light.

Saturday, October 8, 1983

The first full day of the new era.

The morning routine was like a pantomime—going through the motions while my mind raced in continually changing directions. It was a pattern of behavior that would become familiar in the days that followed.

On Saturday mornings we allow the children to watch cartoons until Ashley leaves for ballet class. The same applied now. I took Ashley to ballet and then walked to the farmers' market a block from our house to purchase cider, cheese, and apple pie. At the market I talked briefly with neighbors.

As difficult as it was to go through the process of human contact and small talk, it was a lot better than no contact. Just sitting around and allowing these events to swirl around in my head was exhausting.

We decided to take advantage of the beautiful fall day and do something outdoors. Niki phoned my cousin Theodora (Toots) Tsongas, an epidemiologist at OSHA, to invite her and her boyfriend and fellow epidemiologist, Bob Nugent, to join us. We had been close to Toots and Bob ever since we came to Washington. We called them that day because they are totally irreverent and can always provide comic relief. Or as Ashley once said, "Toots and Bob are a lot of fun, for relatives." In addition, given their professions, we could tell them about the diagnosis and get an intelligent reaction as well as sympathy. Over time they would prove to be our most solid sources of good information and judgment.

We decided to take a picnic lunch to the Potomac River near

Great Falls as soon as Ashley got out of ballet class. Bob had to prepare for his Ph.D. orals and could not come.

While waiting I began to play Trashman, which is the Commodore 64 equivalent of Pac Man for home computers. The game had been the source of some interest for weeks, and now I found myself using it as a way of focusing my mind on a competitive, fast-reacting situation. It worked. You cannot play a home video game like that and not concentrate. In the following two weeks, I would play it for hours.

Toots arrived with a distant relative from Greece who was visiting her. We got into the cars and drove out to Great Falls, found a parking spot, and proceeded down the embankment to the edge of the Potomac River.

The sunshine was brilliant, the river was beautiful, and I was surrounded by a perfect natural environment and a perfect family. While Niki and Toots and the girls went about the picnic chores, our relative from Greece bore down on me. He was an American-educated engineer and an aggressive seeker of business opportunities. Having a United States senator to yourself is a rare chance to penetrate the American scene and perhaps to elicit suggestions for new avenues of enterprise. As the children and Niki and Toots played by the river's edge, I lay on a blanket and weathered his conversation. Normally this would not bother me, but under the circumstances it seemed like a kind of torture.

After enduring as much as I could, I got up and wandered down to the others. I wanted to get away, but he followed me there. I was about to say something exceedingly nasty, so I jumped across some rock ledges to a large boulder too far out in the river for easy access by my pursuer. It worked, and I lay on the large rock basking in the sun and allowed my mind to run free. How many sunny days would I have? How beautiful and how timeless the river; how transitory all this really is.

Finally I turned around and looked back to where Niki and Toots and the children were playing. That moment is seared in my mind, because it was the first time I envisioned them without me. On the rock, too far away to be part of them, I watched a scene which could easily have occurred with me gone.

At first my reaction was sadness. How wonderful they all were —and how much I yearned to be there always. I realized that these scenes had taken place through the last nine years when I was away in Massachusetts or somewhere else and had not been able to partake of this magic. Not because of cancer, but because of a priority. Now my political schedule was utterly secondary.

If I was to be taken from this scene permanently, the same activities would occur—except I would be observing not from a rock but from somewhere else. Around me were other families, some with fathers. I wondered how much those fathers really appreciated those moments. Where the hell were the fathers who were not there? What could be more important than being here with their families?

Eventually my moroseness gave way to a new awareness. I was looking at a very workable unit. Niki and Toots were good friends—both being more open and giving and communicative than I am. They were clearly able to enjoy each other instinctively. The children were playing (Ashley had brought a friend along), and I was warmed by their ease.

They might be repeating this day in the future and having a great time without me. They all had their lives to live and too much to offer to be imprisoned by prolonged grief. The thought possessed me. I had grown up without my mother, but the love of caring people had filled the void. The same would happen to my family. Of course, there would be loneliness and a sense of loss, but there were too many friends and relatives, particularly back in Massachusetts, to allow them to be alone. So this scene would be repeated in a thousand variations and they would be happy.

My initial shock at this realization was accompanied by self-pity. The more I thought about it, however, the more I found this reality filling me with comfort. I felt pleasure in having married Niki and how she had been the glue of our family. I was almost tearfully grateful to Toots for caring as she did about Niki and the children.

Too much to absorb.

I stepped off the boulder, went over to them, and ventured out to another boulder a jump away. Ashley and her friend, Kate, joined me, and we sat on the rock as the water rolled past us.

"Isn't this beautiful, Ashley?" I said, my voice filled with a sense of awe and affection.

"Yes, it is. Daddy, can we eat? Kate and I are starved."

The wonder would have to wait.

I slipped going off the rock and got wet. Everyone roared. I have always had great confidence in my physical coordination and condition. My slip into the water after Ashley and Kate's effortless jumps to dry land was especially pleasurable to the spectators. The fact that Niki and Toots could laugh at me so easily and so unabashedly, given what they knew, was delightful. Normalcy—wonderful normalcy.

In time the picnic ended, but only after I had stuffed myself. I had had little or no appetite for the past few days, but the pleasures of the occasion brought back my hunger with a vengeance.

We returned home, and Toots and our relative stayed. He returned to his train of conversation, and it soon drove me upstairs for a purported nap—a pretty feeble excuse at 6:00 P.M. Lying in the bedroom by myself was too depressing, so I went down to busy myself doing the laundry. My Greek relative watched this United States senator walk by with a laundry basket full of soiled clothes when I was supposed to be napping. I will never know what crossed his mind, but his impression of the American political system was bound to be forever warped.

That evening both Ashley and Katina had friends over for the night. I put Molly to bed, and she asked me for water, which is her usual way of eking out a few more moments of activity. She drank the entire cup and said, "Tanks." So we hugged and kissed, and my heart took flight.

Later that night Niki and I phoned her sisters in California. The calls reinforced the realization that telling people you have cancer is quite unlike telling people you have other serious ailments. The word is terrifying. It doesn't mean illness. It implies death.

Sunday, October 9, 1983

Sunday found us trying to climb out of our emotional darkness. By midmorning we would drive the three blocks to St. Alban's Episcopal Church to attend services.

My grandfather had been one of the leaders of the Greek Orthodox church in Lowell, and I grew up surrounded by the church and the social community it embraced. My children have been baptized in the Greek church and have Greek names in addition to their English names. Father John Sarantos is my priest in Lowell, and he and his wife are Ashley's godparents. Katina and Molly's godparents are Greek Orthodox as well. Niki, however, is an Episcopalian, and we have attended services at an Episcopal church. We have felt that the children should be exposed to both churches and be free to make their own choices when they reach an appropriate age.

In Washington we found it difficult to interest the children in the Orthodox church, because they do not understand Greek (although they would later start taking Greek lessons), and so in the summer of 1983 we decided to try the closest Episcopal church, St. Alban's.

St. Alban's is very much an establishment church, nestled in the shadow of the imposing National Cathedral. It is small and genteel and intellectual and quite unlike what we had been used to. But it had three obvious advantages for our family. The service was in English, so Ashley and Katina could understand; there were child-care facilities for Molly; and there were women ministers. In our household, women's rights were a passion shared by all, and the sight of female acolytes and ministers had a profound effect, especially on Ashley.

The fit was natural, and I enjoyed knowing that on weekends when I was away Niki and the girls could go there comfortably. Now in our time of need, St. Alban's was to be our spiritual haven.

On that Sunday Niki and I found ourselves swimming in emotions in the church—trying to sort everything out. We weren't just attending services, we needed them. That Sunday would begin the process of our coming to grips with the value of institutionalized worship—the act of churchgoing being a regular and systemized opportunity to renew one's search for faith. Within the dark wooded confines of St. Alban's, we were able to begin the task of enlarging the spiritual foundation of our lives.

After the services, we skipped the adult forum session at the church while Ashley and Katina attended Sunday school. We gathered up Molly and walked across to the National Cathedral to wander in its "Bishop's Garden." We often took the children to this lovely retreat after a heavy dinner; it was only a ten-minute walk from our house. On this Sunday, it served as a retreat of a different sort.

We sat on an old wooden bench at the edge of the lawn with the cathedral behind us and nothing but trees and greenery in front. Molly ran around the lawn, trying to start a game of hide and seek.

Niki and I spoke about the future. The time had come for some decisions. We talked and talked and talked, and when we had finished, several things were clear.

First, we would return to Massachusetts. That was where home was—and would always be. Lowell was where people cared

about us—my title notwithstanding. The affection for and interest in our family was genuine and not dependent upon my being
in the Senate.

We had made many friendships in Washington and would
work to keep them going. But most of Washington views people
through the prism of title. Did our friends like me for my office?
One could never know. And this doubt always had a corrosive
effect upon our feelings. We have never felt rooted in Washington. Just the opposite. We had maintained a large house in Lowell
at great financial cost—it was a way of making sure we had a
permanent home. In addition, after nine years, we felt we had
experienced Washington fully. By moving from Alexandria to
the Cleveland Park section of the capital in January 1982, we had
become part of the "real" Washington. We had enjoyed both
places, but the Cleveland Park house was nicer, and we particularly felt comfortable with our neighbors and the area public
school.

Second, we decided to sell the Washington house and use the
proceeds to buy a place on Cape Cod. It would give us something
to look forward to each summer as well as be a sound investment.
Third, Niki would return to law school and finish getting her
degree. The need to have her career path in place was obvious.
If she was going to be the breadwinner someday, the law degree
was essential. Would Boston University Law School readmit her
after all the years away?

Finally, we decided that it made no sense for me to run again
for the Senate, although the reelection mechanism was already in
full gear. It didn't matter anymore. What we were dealing with
here was life—not issues, not job satisfaction, but the question of
how long I would live. Political ambition and reelection strategy
seemed almost juvenile in their innocence and irrelevance. The
priority cards had been drastically shuffled.

Until two weeks before, like many in the Senate, I had occasionally mused about national office. Now I no longer wanted
to run the country. I just wanted to live in it.

Another reason was purely logistical. If the family was back in Massachusetts, I could not live in Washington by myself three or four nights a week. The entire discussion was cool and rational, interspersed with moments of dismay about the medical reality and moments of laughter as Molly rambled in and out of the garden paths and hideaways.

We returned to St. Alban's, retrieved Ashley and Katina, and went to Baskin-Robbins on Connecticut Avenue for ice cream. This weekly tradition made no sense nutritionally, coming just before lunch, but it was nice nonetheless.

That afternoon I sought some mind-absorbing activity. Many more games of Trashman and I would be rightfully accused of having been reduced to "inoperative." So I started painting some bookcases that Niki had bought at a garage sale a few days before.

On the porch, I began the job, listening to the New England Patriots play the Baltimore Colts. The game was exasperating (the Patriots lost), but the play-by-play engaged my mind. Going back to Massachusetts would allow me to pursue this sports addiction while at the same time keeping me off "the subject." It was all clear now. The imagery made me laugh. I would spend my life watching or listening to the Red Sox—Patriots—Celtics —Bruins—and then playing Trashman on the home computer between games.

Dennis Kanin came over with Carol and their three-week-old son, Zachary. Dennis was the most methodical, businesslike campaign manager and administrative assistant imaginable. It was hard to think of him as a father, with a child competing for his time.

But Dennis had been transformed into the most doting and single-minded father I have ever encountered. Indeed, for much of late September and October he insisted on working at home so he could be near Zachary.

Finally the others went inside to make chocolate-chip cookies, and Dennis and I got down to business. I told him I was not going to run again, and my emotions once more broke out. Although my decision would affect him directly, he made no comment on the politics. Instead he argued softly with me on the medical prognosis. I had focused on the worst-case scenario, since everything seemed to be on that track. He took a more optimistic view, but he didn't reach me. The only benefit from this discussion was that after a decade of fighting political wars together and his managing my office, I told him how much I appreciated his talents, his loyalty, and his friendship. I am just terrible at that kind of statement, but it seemed to come naturally under the circumstances.

Later that evening I had an occasion to experience how strangely the mind works.

After we had put the children to bed, Katina woke up and cried out. I went into her room to see what the matter was. It turned out to be a nightmare, and she was soon asleep again. But as I lay next to her on the bed, I wondered whether I had done right in responding to her cry. Would it have been better not to help her, to let her begin to learn to do without me? Was I serving her long-term interests by reinforcing an emotional dependence on me that might soon be cut off? Or was I doing the right thing by trying to give her a foundation of affection? I wondered about fathers who died in wars and never had a chance to experience the birth of their children. I had witnessed the delivery of all three of my children and had shared life with them. How did a soldier feel dying in Germany, or Guadalcanal, or Vietnam, or Korea, or Lebanon knowing that back home was a child he had never seen? I was wallowing in my misfortunes, and yet compared to most people, I was much blessed. I thought about my successful political career and the four people in my house. Was there anyone I would change places with? No. What was I complaining about?

What was I complaining about? The goddam cancer . . . that's what. I had been blessed up to now, but what about from here on in?

Monday, October 10, 1983

On Columbus Day we drove out to Harpers Ferry, West Virginia. Usually, if we have a free weekend, we stay close to home. Now we were being compulsive about activity.

The drive and day were interesting enough as a diversion. I watched the children at play—not a normal observing, but more a devouring—trying to cast each moment in bronze so that it would be more precious, more memorable.

Why hadn't I ever felt this way before? Had I thought I would live forever? Had I believed they would be young forever? Why had I spent so many weekends over the past nine years away from them?

I wondered about fathers—and mothers—who never felt this way because they never had to face a similar crisis. How much they were missing.

This would be my clearest remembrance of Harpers Ferry, because it was so striking and because it has never left me.

On our return, I busied myself with painting the remaining bookshelves and my old standby, doing the laundry.

Tomorrow was the full report, and I didn't want to think about it.

Chapter 3

Details

Tuesday, October 11, 1983

I awoke and went downstairs to see if the paint had dried on the bookshelves. It had, and I carried them to their places. Molly was especially pleased that her bedroom toys and books would be put in some order—she is the only one in the family with neatness genes.

I then walked Katina to school and took Molly to her play group at a friend's house. Ashley was sick and would not go to school. Niki drove her to exercise class all bundled up so she would not get in my way . . . what way?

I pulled the now defunct Massachusetts schedule out of my briefcase and looked at it.

7:00–7:40 A.M.	*Drive to Boston [I had planned to spend the previous night in Lowell.]*
7:45–8:50 A.M.	*Breakfast with the Harvard Business Club at the Harvard Club, 1 Federal Street, through Bill Crozier*

9:00–12:00 noon	*Travel time to Pittsfield*
12:00–12:30 P.M.	*Meeting with board of directors of Pittsfield Central City Development Corporation, through Bob Quaptrochi*
12:30–1:45 P.M.	*Luncheon with Pittsfield Development Corporation at the Country Club, 150 people*
1:45–2:45 P.M.	*Travel time to Springfield*
3:00–3:30 P.M.	*Meet with superintendent of schools, others to discuss the Springfield-Monsanto teacher corporation*
3:30–4:00 P.M.	*Meet with retrained teachers, press invited*
4:00–5:15 P.M.	*Travel time to Athol*
5:00–5:45 P.M.	*Orange-Athol Chamber of Commerce and selectmen at Knights of Columbus Hall*
5:45–6:45 P.M.	*Dinner with Athol leaders*
7:00–9:30 P.M.	*Athol Town Meeting, Town Hall, Mike Davis to introduce P.T.*
9:30–10:00 P.M.	*Meet with unions after meeting*
10:00–11:00 P.M.	*Return to Lowell*

All these events had been canceled on Friday. How suspicious would everyone be? Would they begin to ask questions, would the press start to make inquiries?

Peter Aucella of my Boston staff would have to tell the Harvard Business Club I wasn't feeling well and had to remain at home. What about Bill Crozier, the president of BayBanks, who had been a supporter for several years? The breakfast was a favor to Bill, who wanted to expose me to this group of conservatives. He would clearly not appreciate the lack of notice, since the attendees would have only him to blame. He would be in an embarrassing situation, but what was the choice? I simply could not have phoned him and been sure I didn't sound so strange as to make him suspicious. Better that he be angry at me for a while. (As it turned out, his reaction was just the opposite. Bill would later ask one of my staff why I was angry at *him*.)

The Pittsfield event was the time bomb. I had had a visit scheduled in that city in February only to have it canceled by a snowstorm. A replacement appearance in September was also dropped at the last moment so that I could attend Senator Henry Jackson's funeral in Seattle. Now a third wipeout. Bob Quaptro-chi would be furious. I was supposed to be the senator whose major passion was downtown development, and as far as Pittsfield was concerned, I set up appearances only to withdraw without giving sufficient notice to undo all the preparations.

This would be seen as outrageous insensitivity. Would Pitts-field's *Berkshire Eagle* assign a reporter to smell out the several cancellations?

The Springfield event could be rescheduled.

Athol was a different matter. I had not made a public appearance there during my first five Senate years. I had driven into Athol to inspect its downtown before, but no one had known of my presence. The several events in Athol were an attempt to make up for past neglect. The local leaders were excited, since Athol's remote location in north-central Massachusetts meant that state politicians were infrequently seen.

How would the people in Athol react? Chances were they would write me off as just another Boston pol (even though

Lowell is not Boston) who really didn't give a damn about them. But what if they got so upset as to contact Boston TV or the *Globe* or *Herald*?

No, that was not likely. Instead they would be hurt. That gave me less to worry about, but it also made me feel like a villain.

I told Dennis to cancel Wednesday's events as well. Chris would have to tell people I didn't feel well. There would probably be more tests, so it was better to do it now than at the last minute.

Among Wednesday's events were meetings with John LaWare, president of the Shawmut Bank, Ken Himmel of Urban Investment, and Mort Zuckerman of *The Atlantic,* a carpenter's union endorsement, and dinner with former governor Edward King and his transportation secretary, Jim Carlin.

Postponing these appointments to another time would present no difficulty. All were busy people and accustomed to schedule changes.

There was also a fundraiser in Lincoln at the home of George Hatsopoulos. It was a $500-a-person event attracting high-tech executives and wealthy Greek-Americans. Postponing it would be a mess. But the guests were by definition friends, so in time they would understand. But would they talk about it to others?

My big concern Wednesday was a debate between the two winners of the Tuesday primary for Boston's mayoralty. It was an immediate confrontation between the exhausted primary winners, barely eight hours after they knew whether they had survived the first vote. It would be high drama, and every politician in the state would be there. Every politician, that is, except me. The sponsoring organization was the Boston *Herald*—and I had been personally invited by editor Shelley Cohen (an old friend from the Lowell *Sun*) to sit at the table of Robert Page, the paper's new publisher.

When I didn't show up, what would all these newspaper people think? Would they be so caught up in the excitement of the mayoralty contest that my absence would not be noted? It was possible. But more likely there would be questions about why I would pass up such an opportunity to get to know the publisher of the *Herald* and why I would not be present at such a highly charged political gathering with my own reelection efforts already underway. Would the editors ask the Washington bureaus what was going on?

I had hardly ever ducked an event in my years in office. It would be highly unusual.

Then there were the appearances for Thursday, Saturday, and Sunday. They were still intact.

Enough, already.

I could not worry about every possible incident. Massachusetts political events were far away. The phone call from Dr. Veach would come this afternoon, and that was close indeed.

The Trashman cassette was still in the computer, so I started playing some games. The concentration on the game soon gave way to a disgust at my behavior—a forty-two-year-old man sitting in front of a television set manipulating a joystick to see if he could prevent the "flies" from eating the "trash truck" before it picked up all of the "pellets" and "trashcans."

I slammed down the joystick and shut off the computer. Yes, I had been dealt a bitter blow, but I was acting in a way that no one, including myself, could respect. My mind was assuming a fetal position. My concern about Dr. Veach's impending call was overcome by anger at myself.

Damn it, I told myself, start acting like a functioning human being.

I took out some tools and went upstairs to remove the window from the bathroom. The pane had been broken for two years, and we were chilled every winter as the cold air beat against the cellophane we had installed as a "temporary" fix. I also took the cracked window panel from the front storm door, which had been broken several months before. There had never been enough time to do these chores until now.

The nearest glass shop was in Bethesda. Driving up Wisconsin Avenue, I was getting closer to Bethesda Naval Hospital. This famous Washington avenue had now taken on a symbolism for me, and I had to suppress the urge to find a glass shop in another direction.

Returning home with the panel, I met Niki and Ashley coming back from exercise class. We decided to stay out of the house and keep busy. We took rugs to a downtown cleaner, bought paint on Connecticut Avenue for Molly's ceiling (the paint would remain in the can until we hired a painter five months later), and shopped for groceries. By the time we returned home, I was in a better frame of mind.

Soon after a late lunch, the phone rang. It was Dr. Veach.

I went upstairs to the bedroom. Before picking up the phone, I took a white cardboard shirt back from my dresser drawer and wrote at the top, "Veach, October 11, 2:20 P.M."

"Hello."

"Senator Tsongas, this is Dr. Veach. I have the final test results."

The Friday findings were confirmed. It was nodular poorly differentiated lymphoma—a non-Hodgkin's lymphoma.

The type was indolent. They would have to test the enlarged lymph nodes to determine treatment.

There were three possibilities: no treatment, treatment, and very aggressive treatment. It was still an area of controversy. The lymph nodes might respond to treatment or might not. Indeed, treatment might not be necessary, but lymph nodes would have to be watched.

Then came the words that exploded in my head.

"There is no evidence that treatment affects survival," Dr. Veach said. "This form of lymphoma has never been cured."

Never been cured.

I had to force myself to listen to the words that followed. He talked about what was going on at the National Cancer Institute, including attempts at very aggressive chemotherapy, but nothing had yet succeeded in curing patients. If the lymphoma was still indolent, I would be examined every month or two. When it became systematic and aggressive, there would be pain, swelling, fever, sweats, chills, and a sense of malaise.

Never been cured.

It would be necessary to check into Bethesda Hospital for a series of tests. The doctors would go into my hip and extract some bone marrow to determine the extent of the disease. There would be a CAT scan of my chest and abdomen. And there would be the usual chest x-rays, blood tests, etc.

Never been cured.

We agreed that I would go to Bethesda the next morning and begin the tests. Veach's voice was contained, professional, clinical.

I hung up the phone and began the rapid descent into despair.

Never been cured.

What was there to fight for? At least with Hodgkin's, while you would be ravaged by chemotherapy for a while, there would be a good chance at cure.

What was there to hope for? A crushing sense of frustration swept over me. What was there to pray for?

I hit bottom.

The next two hours I was bathed in emotions. I told Niki what Dr. Veach had said. Or rather, I told her what I thought he had said.

At one point, I tried to be stoic about having incurable cancer.

"You know, Niki, I don't really care that I won't live long enough to see my grandchildren," I said, resorting to sheer falsehood in a headlong search for solace.

"Well, I do," she came back.

Of course she did. And of course I did.

Niki steered me with compassion through my dejection and futility. I wanted to live, and I wanted a chance to fight for my life. Please, God.

After the first wave of emotion passed, I phoned Dr. Canellos.

Toots and Bob had researched lymphoma, and almost every article they found had Canellos's name on it. If we were going to move to Massachusetts, I needed to have someone there to assume responsibility for my treatment. Besides, medical expertise abounded in Boston.

He came on the phone.

"How was Israel?" I asked. I knew he had recently returned from there.

The question was an absurdity. I had just been told that the cancer coursing through my body had never been cured. I was reaching out for help in desperation, and the first words out of my mouth were "How was Israel?"

Imagine yourself in his shoes. You are a renowned expert in cancer research and treatment. In your absence you have been contacted by your senator because he has cancer. You know that on this day the final diagnosis will be given to the senator, but you already know it's lymphoma. The senator calls. You have never met or spoken with him. He gets on the phone and says, "How was Israel?"

In my despair I still felt compelled to be cool and seemingly removed. Instead of screaming, "Please save me," I had said, "How was Israel?"

"Israel was interesting," he informed me. "Now, what's going on?" he asked. His expertise was in medicine, not foreign travel.

I repeated what Dr. Veach had told me from the cardboard shirt back. When I finished, I turned it over and wrote, "October 11, 1983. 5:00 P.M. Canellos." I wanted to write it all down, mainly because when I repeated it to Niki, I wanted to be exact. Also, writing down the diagnosis made it seem more real. Ironically, it would be months before I could get myself to look at that cardboard again.

Canellos listened to my recitation without comment. Then he began a description of the disease from his perspective. There were two theories: no treatment and aggressive treatment. The disease waxes and wanes, so I should be aware that the lymph nodes could expand and contract. (Mine had not.)

He had been involved in a new technique that was a kind of bone-marrow approach. The first patient experiments had recently begun at the Dana-Farber Cancer Institute.

As for the next day's tests, he had full confidence in Bethesda. I should expect that the disease would show up in my bone-marrow cells, my other lymph nodes, and my spleen.

"The disease is not life-threatening in its present form. It can go on for years in its indolent state. Excuse me—Dr. Veach is on the other line. Let me take his call, and you and I will talk again later."

"Oh, okay. Thank you."

Was he supposed to call back? I didn't know.

I looked at my notes and repeated the conversation to Niki. Not only was Canellos more clinically optimistic, but his voice had been hopeful in its tone and cadence. Its effect was like a shot of adrenaline. I could feel myself being lifted out of the despair —not pulling myself out, but being lifted out. Two and a half hours earlier I had been in hell; now I was back on earth. Niki responded to my new frame of mind. I bounced off the bed eager to do something.

Toots and Bob came to check in. We talked like four experts on lymphoma. They stayed for dinner, and later Katina and I played cards ("crazy eights") by the fire. She won when I let her win, and she won when I tried not to let her win. Her laughter delighted me. I wondered how often she had laughed before and how seldom I took notice of it. It was a marvelous sound, and I hugged her, crushingly.

"Daddy, you're wrecking the cards!"

Ashley, Bob, and I played Trashman on the computer. They had both been hooked for weeks anyway, and we were competing again. Bob had held the previous record at around 24,000, but Ashley had recently broken it with 31,000. She was exceedingly proud of herself and couldn't wait to tell Bob he had fallen by the wayside.

For two hours we went at it. For me, it was the same old game, but now it was with people I cared about, not an escape from horror. I took the joystick with gusto and eventually set a new record at 33,000. Deriving great pleasure from breaking the mark of your nine-year-old daughter is the mark of a warped mind. But this was different, I told myself; and there was no reason to feel unduly guilty.

At 9:30, Toots and Bob left, and I went to National Airport to pick up Thaleia from her Boston flight.

The giddiness had worn off, and I was back to a kind of middle state of composure. There wouldn't be a normal day of quiescent emotions for a long time.

Wednesday, October 12, 1983

The dread had sat on my bed all night and welcomed me to the morning. It was day number one in my new life as a human being with cancer. And since it was incurable, there would never be a morning when I would wake up without it.

I walked Ashley and Katina to school, this time going down Macomb Street to 34th. Molly came with us, and the October sun shone through the trees. They walked a few paces ahead of me, and I watched them achingly. Especially Molly. Ashley and Katina were doing just fine. They were well adjusted, liked each other as much as siblings can, and were good students. They drove us nuts occasionally, but their physical and emotional health was good, and they seemed to be intellectually capable. Molly had just turned two in July. Would I live long enough to be involved in her future? I looked back, and Niki was standing on the lawn watching us walk away. It was a poignant moment. Niki's expression was that of a mother observing her now vulnerable husband and their three young children. How would it be in the future? In a way it was like the time when I was on the rock on the Potomac River looking back at her. It was the intensity of a moment framed by the people and the sunshine, and capturing the meaning of what our life had been.

She watched us as we slowly disappeared down the street. Whenever I glanced back she was still there.

The thought of returning to Bethesda in an hour depressed me. After leaving Ashley and Katina at school, I returned with Molly, holding her in my arms far too tightly to make any sense. It had been thirteen days since I had felt the lump, and except for a few periods of sanity and relief, I did not have much to be proud of when I reviewed my mental response to my illness. Here I was, alive on a sunny fall day with a loving child in my arms, and what was I doing? Wondering whether I would live to be forty-three in February.

It was obvious what was happening.

I was totally discounting the positive and hopeful information. All the talk about normal infections and cat-scratch syndrome and even Hodgkin's disease had turned out to be false hopes. I had groped at them, and they were but illusions.

There would be no more groping. I would accept the worst case and learn to deal with it. The indolent lymphoma would become aggressive, and it could not be cured. That was the bottom line, and the sooner I accepted it, the sooner the roller coaster would stop.

At the hospital Dr. Shen conducted the bone-marrow tests. While the equipment was being set up, he mentioned a new experiment at the National Cancer Institute involving the creation of antibodies to the cancerous cells. He described the theory in some detail, but none of it stuck in my mind. I could absorb surface small talk and marginally substantive discussion, but serious, technical material was beyond me.

He went on to explain the nature of the test. The purpose was to determine whether the disease had spread to the bone marrow.

Taking out a model of a hip, he showed me where he would

bore in with a drill and reach into the marrow. He would give me a local anesthetic, but it would have no effect once we hit the bone itself. "It will be very painful, Senator."

"It's only pain," I replied. My mind was on more dreadful thoughts.

I lay down on the operating table, and Shen injected an anesthetic into each side of my upper central hip. When the anesthetic took hold, he cut into me to reach the nearby bone. He then began boring into the bone with the hand drill. He pressed hard on me and twisted the drill turn by turn. I cannot describe the pain. When he got in far enough, he used a suction device to extract the bone-marrow specimen. I groaned involuntarily. This part really hurt like hell, and I couldn't suppress my reaction. "Oh, God."

During the procedure and the identical one on the other side, only some thirty minutes passed.

As I lay face down on the table, two thoughts dominated my consciousness.

First, I realized how temporary and contained was the pain. It was the worst I had ever experienced, but surely less than what others had undergone. I thought about Niki and the hours of pain during childbirth. I thought of Jacobo Timerman, the Argentine publisher who was brutally tortured because he was Jewish. I thought about the thousands of people in prison cells around the world at that moment, experiencing continual and worse suffering, inflicted by people with hate in their hearts, and without loved ones down the hall ready to take them home when it was over.

For years I had been active in human-rights movements, but on that table I felt a glimpse of the horror of prisoners of conscience. Multiply my pain a thousandfold day after day and remove any serious hope of escape from their torturers—how could they stand it? Why didn't their minds crack? How utterly alone they must feel.

The second thought was very different. As Shen extracted the bone marrow the second time, I said the Lord's Prayer silently to myself. When I finished, I tried to repeat the Twenty-third Psalm, but I couldn't remember it entirely.

In my desolation I had to reach deep into my beliefs. Those beliefs had never been sorely needed before—not like this. Now it would be different. God would be more a part of my life, no matter what happened. This was not a revelation or born-again experience. Not at all. Just a realization that while I had taken myself this far in life and done quite well, from here on in I needed to recognize who was guiding me. I had to be more aware that one does not go through life without God's presence.

The Navy attendants helping Shen tried to divert my attention by talking about the Boston Red Sox. I would resurface from my thoughts to answer their questions and respond to their banter, and then resubmerge in my various musings.

Finally, Dr. Shen finished up. I got myself off the table slowly and looked at him. He was sweating profusely.

"Why are *you* sweating?" I asked. "I'm the one that was being drilled into."

"Because I was doing the work," he said wearily.

With the procedure completed, the absence of pain was a relief that again caused a sense of euphoria. We returned to Dr. Veach's office, and Niki joined us. We talked further about various medical matters, and then Veach took me to the new building to be admitted.

I lay down on my bed, and Niki and I spoke about the same things we had discussed in the Bishop's Garden the Sunday before.

"Well, what do you think we should do about leaving the Senate and moving back to Massachusetts?" I asked.

"I feel the same way," she replied.

"So do I."

Nothing had changed. The plans for our future were the same.

After Niki left on errands, Dr. Shen came in to report that he had looked at the bone-marrow specimen through a microscope. It was all exceedingly preliminary, but he had not spotted any cancerous cells. There would be more sophisticated analyses, but at least on this level nothing was there.

Nothing there?

There's nothing there. It has not spread to my bone marrow. My God, there's actually good news. For once I had not lost a throw of the dice.

Once more he tried to explain the antibody experiment to me, but it still went over my head.

He then talked about the lymphoma in its various aspects.

I was now ready for the question I had been unable to pose before.

"How long can I expect to live?"

That is *the* question, of course. All of the tests and diagnoses and theories are only relevant to the extent that they relate to your life—and how long your life will continue. The technical and medical details had been the entire focus of attention. It was time to confront the only news that counted.

"How long can I expect to live?"

The question made Dr. Shen very nervous. He was a doctor and knew the various nuances and unknowns. The prognosis could be almost anything, and here was a public figure demanding to know how long he would live.

Well, he said, there are many possible developments. He went into a long discourse about the fact that the tests had not been completed, that statistical data on others with this disease were incomplete, that an average was just that and might well not apply to me. He was trying to be realistic and to present the entire argument why an answer to my question would be almost meaningless. I gave him no escape.

Finally and very reluctantly, he said, "The statistical average for life expectancy in similar cases is about eight years."

Eight years!

My heart leaped. Anyone at age forty-two told about such a prognosis would be crushed. Not me. I was elated.

Eight years!

Ashley would be seventeen, Katina would be fourteen, and Molly would be ten. Molly would remember me.

Niki would have finished law school and been in practice for five years. We would have been married for twenty-two years. Not enough, but under the circumstances, not all that bad.

Eight years! I would indeed live to be forty-three. I would, in fact, get to another decade.

Dr. Shen tried to qualify the answer, to explain that it was just an average, that it could be less, and it could be more.

I didn't care. Now I had an honest-to-goodness number to focus on. And the number was higher than I had expected.

He also said he would probably recommend a course of no treatment, but that was subject to further tests and discussion with other doctors. None of this seemed to matter. Eight years was what mattered.

When Dr. Shen left, I called Niki with the good news. She was shocked. Her reaction stunned me, and I realized the distance between our assumptions. I had been the pessimist lusting after every bit of negative data. She had been the optimist ready to do battle until I was cured.

Dennis walked in while I was on the phone. When Niki and I finished, I told him the same news. Eight years. My obvious pleasure clearly surprised him. I explained that compared to my fears eight years was almost infinity. I'm sure he thought I was a basket case, and those eight years would probably best be spent in a psychiatric ward.

We went on to talk about how to stop the campaign, what expenses we had incurred, and whether or not I would be left with a debt and if so how much.

Then we spoke about January 1985. What would we do?

I was concerned about the fact that when I left the Senate I would not be able to obtain health or life insurance. Dr. Shen had said that any coverage would be the policy amount divided by my life expectancy. It would be prohibitive. There might be an economic catastrophe ahead for me—and for Niki—and for the children.

Dennis made a few calls, and the information was not good. It seemed that there would be either no coverage or coverage at prohibitive rates. The prospect of having no insurance was sobering.

We then got down to the business of organizing my retirement from politics. We certainly had a lot of experience about how to enter a political contest. We even had experience thinking about what I would say were I defeated along the way.

My old political instincts were still intact. Giving up a Senate seat now seemed very significant, despite the overwhelming nature of other matters. With Dennis, I could appreciate what I was doing. The loss of capacity to influence events, the coming to an end of a political career, the removing of oneself from the great issues—all this was not a casual decision. It was to be done, but not done lightly.

In addition, since it would be my last hurrah, it should be done well.

The timing was important. The tests wouldn't be over until the end of the week. I would not announce my decision on Friday or Saturday for Saturday or Sunday coverage—especially Saturday. Making the poorly circulated Saturday papers is useless, and Sunday's edition is too big. You either get ignored or get lost. A Sunday press conference was equally out of the question, because the best and most experienced reporters don't work on the weekends. Monday would be the first opportunity.

To announce on Monday would also be best since I would first have to tell my Washington and Boston staffs. I would convene the Washington staff at 8:00 A.M., take a midmorning plane to Boston, meet with the Boston staff at 12:30, and then hold the press conference about 3:00. It would give everyone who worked for me a chance to hear the news directly, while the public announcement would still make the six-o'clock news.

The ongoing campaign would probably end up in debt if we stopped now, because many of the expenses, such as the computer and the direct mail, were up-front costs. At the end of the 1978 campaign, our debt had been more than $100,000. I didn't want to repeat that situation. How much could I raise as a lame duck? Not a hell of a lot.

Dr. Veach came in to describe the tests scheduled for the next day, and to discuss lymphoma. He continued to be very clinical and guarded in his approach.

The cool professionalism of the doctors at Bethesda was beginning to have a counterproductive effect. As time went on, I needed to get beyond their analytical posture—to have the people treat me as people. Maybe it was because I was a senator. Maybe it was just characteristic of a well-ordered military hospital. But whatever the reason, the distance was not helpful. I didn't feel like a senator at this time of vulnerability, and being treated like one left me somewhat strung-out.

All this may seem like a very minor point in relation to the medical prognosis, but in the circumstances nothing was minor.

Since the tests were not to resume until the next morning, I got permission to leave the hospital for dinner, on condition that I would return by 10:00 P.M.

Niki, Thaleia, Toots, and I had a drink at the Zebra Room (it was probably my third drink in a year) and then dinner across the street at an Italian restaurant, Piccola Italia. Both places were on Macomb Street just two blocks from our house. We had told the children that I was in Massachusetts, so I could not go that short distance to see them. Being so close but separated from them reminded me again of my mother's situation almost forty years before. I had never before experienced this kind of halfway status. The conversation was as light as the circumstances would allow, but I had no appetite and was very restless.

Earlier in my discussion with Dennis, we had agreed that I should call Nick Rizzo and tell him what was going on. Besides being my chief fundraiser, Nick had been a good friend during the last nine years of my political life. Dennis and Rich and I were liberals, but Nick was a conservative. I doubt that there was one philosophical issue that we agreed upon. In addition, our personal styles could not have been more dissimilar. He was a hard-charging, brusque businessman who was quick to be a friend and quick to remember a slight.

But he was above all loyal, and loyalty knows no ideological constraint. He deserved to know.

So when I got back to Bethesda I called him.

"Hi, Nick. Paul here."

"Where are you? I've been trying to get in touch with you and no one will tell me where you are. You canceled your days up here. What the hell is going on? There's something going on, and I want to know what it is. Where are you? Are you at home?"

"No, I'm in Bethesda Naval Hospital."

"What are you doing there? Are you sick?"

"Well, yes."

"What's wrong? What's going on? Why all the secrecy?"

"Well, Nick, I have cancer."

"You have what!"

"Cancer."

"Are you serious? You're not kidding me?"

"No, I'm not kidding you. I have cancer."

The word did not stick in my throat. I had cancer and that was what it had to be called. I went on to describe it as lymphoma.

"Is it terminal?" he asked.

The question floored me. I was now used to having cancer. But was I also terminal?

"Well, I suppose it could be called terminal. The average survival rate is eight years."

Nick's reaction was one of great thoughtfulness and diplomacy. "You poor bastard." I had to laugh. Vintage Nick, no baloney.

Niki's reaction was just the opposite.

"Everyone's terminal!" she said with great exasperation.

I then told Nick I was not going to run again. He strongly disagreed, arguing that I was putting myself and my family in great financial peril. I was sure to be reelected, and after that I could take it easy and receive all the medical care necessary, not to mention the question of life insurance. "And what the hell would you do if you weren't in the Senate? Who would want someone who's got cancer? Who would hire you? You've got to stay in the Senate, for Niki's sake and the children's."

"Look, Nick, I've made up my mind."

"I'm going to come down there on Sunday, and I want you to promise me you won't tell anyone about your decision. Give me a chance to talk with you face to face. That's all I'm asking."

"All right. But it'll be a waste of time."

"At least it will be my goddam time."

Nick always viewed me as a younger brother who by some mysterious force had managed to achieve high political office. He never lobbied me on any issue, but on organizational, political, and personal matters, he could be insistent. It was occasionally inconvenient, but I never lost sight of the deep personal caring behind that insistence. Once again he would have his say.

Niki and I walked back to the garage, and she drove me back to the entrance of the hospital. Walking into the deserted corridors gave me a sense of two worlds. One was warm, and cared about every part of my life. The other was there only to deal with my disease. I made no judgments—that's just the way it was. I thought about men in other hospitals who were not hugged by a wife—people who were alone, had been alone yesterday, and would be alone tomorrow. If I was having such trouble dealing with all of this, how did others cope? I was not by any means the most ravaged of God's creatures, yet the struggle to accept and to adjust was fierce. What of those who were truly in much worse condition?

I called Dennis and told him of my conversation with Nick. By now the economic impact of quitting had begun to register. The notion of leaving Niki financially strapped with three children to raise and educate weighed very heavily on me. Nick's arguments had their effect. Besides, I loved the Senate, and I had become used to thinking of myself as being able to influence national issues. All the work I had been involved with, from the Chrysler bill to Alaska lands to industrial strategy to foreign policy—all were part of my life. I certainly wouldn't stop caring about issues in January 1985, so there was bound to be an enormous letdown. Dennis admitted that not running might be a serious mistake. It was my decision and he did not want to intrude, but leaving the Senate was something very profound. Had I really thought it all through? Was I making an emotional decision I would later regret?

We discussed the alternative of running and then making fewer speeches and appearances after the election. I promised to think about it and not to make any decision under this kind of stress. We'd leave things as they were and decide later. "One decision stands, however. We will move back to Massachusetts."

I hung up and for the first time considered the second part of Nick's argument. Was it possible that despite all my experience and all I had done, I would not be able to function in a normal working environment outside the Senate because I would be shunned?

It had never entered my mind during these two weeks that cancer was more than a dreaded disease—that it was also a stigma, a kind of modern-day leprosy. Lying in that room I struggled to gain perspective. If I left the Senate under normal circumstances, law firms and universities would seek me out. I would be a "hot item." Would the cancer change that? I couldn't tell. Prolonged periods of incapacity during chemotherapy would be a potential problem that might cause concern. So would an abnormal life expectancy. But how much concern? I just could not tell. And like everything else, when in doubt, presume the worst. And I did.

The phone rang. It was Nick.

He was watching the World Series and wanted to read me a glowing editorial about him in the Lawrence *Eagle Tribune*. He had recently been struggling with phlebitis and was resigning from the presidency of the Lawrence Chamber of Commerce after much yeoman work. The editorial reflected the feelings of a grateful city.

"It's like reading my obituary," he joked. Only Nick could have made such a statement under the circumstances and presumed that we were good enough friends to have it appreciated. I laughed in spite of myself.

We again rehashed the retirement decision, and I told him I would hold off any announcement. I would simply reveal the nature of the illness at the appropriate time and see what happened. Let time sort things out for me.

"You are finally using your head," he said.

I watched some of the World Series, which normally would have interested me, but not now. I turned off the TV and went back to my own thoughts.

I'm forty-two years old. I'm a United States senator.

It wasn't always so.

No one who watched me grow up would have ever figured me for this position. Not even my family. Especially not my family. I was totally apolitical. I had no political interests and no discernible political skills. I was instinctively introspective.

After Lowell High School I went to Dartmouth College and became obsessed with earning my letter in swimming. I got it, but at the price of not having taken advantage of much of Dartmouth's intellectual opportunities.

Then the Peace Corps.

That changed my direction. It would lead to a desire for involvement with a different world.

I didn't know it at the time, but it paved the way to a public life.

I thought about the fateful day when I decided to be a politician. How unlikely it was. It was May of 1968 and I was basking in the sun of St. Thomas in the Virgin Islands. The lushness of the vegetation surrounding Magens Bay contrasted with the cool blue-green waters. It was a scene straight out of a thousand travel posters. Scattered around me were tourists who had spent a small fortune getting to this jewel in the Caribbean to spend a precious few days. It made no difference to me that I was enjoying the same resource and it wasn't costing me a penny—and I had been enjoying it for nine months.

Nine months in paradise. Sun, surf, and constant travel throughout the various Caribbean Islands—St. Thomas, St. Croix, St. John, Antigua, Trinidad, Curaçao, Tobago, Dominica, Puerto Rico, Aruba. Nine months in paradise—and I was bored stiff.

I had taken a job with the Peace Corps as a field coordinator for training volunteers in the Caribbean. I was trying to recapture the deep satisfaction of my two Peace Corps years in Ethiopia in the early 1960s.

Living in an Ethiopian town/village as a teacher was the essence of Peace Corps service. Island hopping in the Caribbean, where tourist opulence and indulgence existed side by side with poverty, was not. I had little contact with the West Indian people, and that created a sense of distance.

I lay on that beach reviewing my life path, and it was certainly getting to be winding.

During my second year at Yale Law, I had decided to take a leave of absence and join the Green Berets in Vietnam as a medic. If I was a medic in a village, I reasoned, I would help the people there and recapture the feeling of worth that I had had in Ethiopia.

It was pointed out to me that Green Beret medics have to kill as well as cure.

After much soul-searching and an aborted attempt to get to Vietnam with AID (Agency for International Development), I was back at Yale Law for my third year. I put away my Vietnamese language primer and my books on guerrilla warfare in Indochina during World War II. I put on my three-piece suit, got a haircut, and signed up for interviews with visiting law firms.

My résumé was not one to gladden the hearts of Wall Street recruiters, since I had taken several courses related to Third World matters instead of Estate Planning, Trusts, Evidence, etc. Yet, Yale Law School is Yale Law School, and we were the chosen ones. These firms were lucky to have a chance to secure the services of any of us.

The first three interviews did not reflect that. The recruiters managed to contain their enthusiasm about my availability. Many of my classmates had better grades and better course selection, but I had lived in Africa for two years, and that made me different —more worldly, more wise, more aware. But there were no offers, no follow-up meetings.

The next interview was with a prominent Boston law firm. The recruiter was a founding partner—a stern, dedicated, talented lawyer. I sat down in the hard chair across the desk from him in one of the cramped rooms set aside for this ritual.

He studied my résumé carefully while I pretended to be comfortable in that three-piece suit which had been purchased two and a half years before.

Finally, he looked up.

"I see where you have been in the Peace Corps," he observed.

"Yes, that's right," I responded, pleased that one of these people had finally paid notice to an experience that I thought had made me valuable.

"Well, it is a transgression that we will overlook," he said graciously, and without humor.

My mouth sagged. I had spent two years in Wolisso teaching students yearning for education. I had learned to speak Amharic, and had done great service to my country. Those people really liked me and I really liked them. And while I ate *injera* and *wat*, lived in difficult conditions, and made eleven cents an hour, this man was eating at Boston's best restaurants and making a fortune.

I walked away from that interview shaking. It was the last one.

I went to the employment bulletin board and looked at the notices. There were the usual New York, Los Angeles, Boston, Washington, Miami, Philadelphia recruitment brochures, with a few long shots thrown in by small city firms hoping to lure a Yalie. I was very discouraged.

One day the bulletin board carried the notice that a former Yale Law graduate was the attorney general of American Samoa in Pago Pago—and he needed an assistant. Housing was provided right off the beach, and it paid $10,000 a year.

Assistant attorney general of American Samoa? Where the hell in the Pacific is it? I ran back to my room and wrote a letter stating my availability. Here was someone who would appreciate my Peace Corps years.

And he did. A return letter expressed real interest.

I told my roommate I would be going to Pago Pago.

"Where?"

"Pago Pago in American Samoa."

"What kind of law do they practice there?"

"How would I know?"

"But where does that lead to?"

"Who cares?"

The application process dragged on, however, and one day I got a call from another Yale Law graduate, David Schimmel, director of Peace Corps training in the West Indies. He knew me from Ethiopia and wanted me to join him as his field coordinator. It paid $8,800 and housing in St. Thomas, the base camp.

My classmates were agonizing about decisions between New York and Washington, and I was agonizing between Pago Pago and the Virgin Islands. I told Schimmel of the Pago Pago opportunity, but he was unsympathetic. He needed a field coordinator right away and gave me a week to decide.

The week passed and the paperwork on Pago Pago had not been resolved. I opted for the West Indies.

Fifteen months later I was on that beach at Magens Bay. The attempt to relive Ethiopia, to return to Mother Peace Corps, had been futile. I had to go on to something else.

But what?

My two summers as a Congressional intern in Washington while in law school had exposed me to politics. I decided I might make a good congressman.

It was presumptuous, naive, absurd.

Yet it happened. Lowell City Council. Middlesex county commissioner. United States congressman. United States senator.

And now a lonely hospital room in Bethesda—and cancer. Incurable cancer. "A meteoric career," the newspapers often said. Meteors burn out, of course.

The past and the future competed for my awareness. My mind raced out of control. I tried to sleep, but the night did not go well.

Thursday, October 13, 1983

Finally, at 4:30 A.M., I was awake for good. For an hour and a half, I lay in the silence and darkness, feeling silent and dark. Should I leave the Senate? How long would I live?

The more I thought about it, the less I could deal with it.

I had to take a more measured approach.

At 6:00 I turned on the light and began to write a diary of the events of the past two weeks. I wanted to put it down on paper so I would never forget. I wanted to reduce it all to paper while it was fresh in my mind, and I bent to the task with relief. If I wrote about my illness, perhaps it would make some sense.

At 7:00 I had a bizarre experience. I was writing the diary, reliving the early days of pain, when the door opened. In came a doctor I had never seen before and would never see again. He told me his name and said, "I know this has been a devastating shock to you, and if there is anything I can do, just let me know." He said a few more sympathetic words and walked out. Good God! I didn't need to know about the devastation, shock. I already knew about that. What I needed was hope, dammit, hope. Don't bury me. Help me to live.

The morning was gray and rainy. It fit my despairing mood perfectly.

I called Niki and recounted the unknown doctor's conversation. She said we had to let the tests be done at Bethesda and then rely upon Canellos in Boston for everything else. I could not lift my morale here. Canellos had interpersonal skills, and I needed that part of medical attention as well. Besides, we would be in Massachusetts full-time anyway.

My struggle of the past week had been emotional more than medical. What I had in me I had in me. That would not change. The tests merely revealed what existed. The only question was how I existed within that reality. To date, my performance had been lamentable. I had to break out of that streak of irresolution. But I knew it would take time.

I went downstairs for an x-ray and sat in a corridor with several other people who were also waiting. Most were quite old, and several were obviously very ill. They were old, and I was relatively young. I felt forlorn and sorry for myself as I sat there in my pajamas. Why couldn't it have happened when I was much older? Oh God, I don't want to be here.

The x-ray attendant was solicitous and tried to cheer me up. It was no use. On the way out, I passed a young man in the corridor who was in terrible agony. I assumed he was in the midst of chemotherapy. It stunned me to see how young he was, and how difficult his situation. I felt ashamed of myself. Next to him in a wheelchair was a bearded, bespectacled man in his thirties who looked like an engineer or a college instructor. As I passed, he smiled at me. It was a smile of genuine warmth and comradeship. I thought he understood what I was feeling.

It was not just me. I was not alone.

Back at the room Niki said I should run for the Senate again. Yesterday I had asked her whether she thought I was giving in to all this, and she had said yes. Now she was starting to force me to fight back. We talked about it, and I began to want to run again. But how would people respond? If I announced I had cancer, would the previously uncontested primary be instantly filled with opponents? Would the general election be more difficult? What would the voters do? How do you get up before your constituents and say, "I have cancer. They probably can't cure it. But never mind, I'm still the same person, so be sure to vote for me again."

Would people be sympathetic or would I now seem maimed, inadequate to the responsibilities of my office?

When Dennis called, he agreed that I should run. We had leafleted Boston on primary night Tuesday, and it had gone well. He then told me about his research on the life-insurance question. If I left, I would still be insurable but the premium would be about $14,000 a year. That was a lot of money, but far less than I had feared. It was at least possible.

By the time Niki left, we had decided that I should stand for reelection. Not because of the insurance, but because I wanted to. I really wanted to. Niki was her usual self, telling me how much my country needed me on issues like arms control and the Third World and the environment and economic development and so on. It was unmitigated hype. She knew it, and I knew it, but I absorbed every word of it. For Niki it would have been much better to go home to Massachusetts and normalcy. But she argued against it. At the time I did not think she was again putting herself second to my career. Instead of being grateful for her kindness, I could only agree to her assessment of my political skills.

So the senator from Massachusetts would remain the senator from Massachusetts. I gave the news to a doctor who came by, and he was pleased. At last, some rational thinking.

I told another doctor, Dr. Ihde, a protégé of Canellos's, that I wanted to deal exclusively with Canellos after the tests. He was very understanding, remarking favorably on Canellos's skill as a medical researcher and as a bedside companion. They would perform the final tests at Bethesda and send copies to Canellos in Boston.

Niki had been right. Bethesda had become synonymous in my mind with the dark period of diagnosis. So many people had been kind, but the place now had a significance I had to put behind me. As I entered the period of treatment, a different kind of place could be very helpful. Knowing I was going to deal with Canellos made the rest of the tests seem like the completion of a chapter and not simply part of an endless process.

Then it was downstairs for a CAT scan. I had drunk six glasses of barium, and the modern technology did its work. How different I felt from the despair at the x-ray department.

Back in the room I called the office, and there was a message from the city manager of Lowell, Joe Tully. For three and a half years we had been putting together a Hilton Hotel/Wang training center complex for downtown Lowell. There had been one problem after another, and the project had consumed enormous amounts of our time.

I phoned him, and we talked about a problem that had arisen, and I promised to try to solve it. When we finished that business, he said, "By the way, are you all right?"

"Yeah, Joe, why do you ask?"

"Well, people are talking and asking whether you are okay."

"It was just a little sickness. The doctor wants me to take it easy, that's all."

I realized that my absences were bound to make people curious eventually. The reality of managing this situation publicly would have to be confronted. I told Chris Naylor to activate the weekend schedule. I wanted to resume a normal routine before the rumors got out of hand.

Working on the Lowell problem gave me a sense of role. Resurrecting my schedule gave me a sense of future. Knowing that Bethesda was coming to an end gave me a sense of closing an era—one that had often gotten the best of me. I wished I had been calmer about all this, but it was too late to change that.

After conferring with the doctors about returning for an angiogram test on Friday, I dressed and drove home. I got to Macomb Street in time to pick Katina up at school.

When Ashley showed up later, she proudly announced that she had beaten my score at Trashman while I was away. I vowed to recapture the record.

I then did the lawn with a vigor that our neighbors had never seen before. Whizzing the mower around as if it were a plastic toy was pure delight. I poured myself into the exertion and derived great pleasure as the sweat rolled down my face. I was alive. Then it was the laundry, Trashman with Ashley (I lost badly), dinner, and a good night's sleep. The roller coaster was going up again.

Chapter 4

Canellos

On Thursday, October 13, when I returned home from Bethesda, the sense of hope and future was surging. I felt I could go on and live a normal life. It had been a nightmare, but by leaving Bethesda I had put the nightmare away for good.

That relief was not a function of a medical prognosis nor a spiritual conviction. It was merely a convenient illusion.

The scar on my groin from the biopsy was still there, and so was the cancer. The cancer was not at Bethesda, it was in me.

Friday, October 14, 1983

The roller coaster leveled off on Thursday, and on Friday morning when I awoke to return to Bethesda for the angiogram, it was headed downhill again.

I knew that like the groin scar the emotional scar would require time to heal. It was the third week of this brave new world, and the healing process was not complete. That did not bother me. My concern was whether the healing had even begun; perhaps the wound was being constantly closed and then re-opened. During the next few hours I would have ample occasion to contemplate the matter.

An angiogram is a fascinating procedure. It is the filling of the lymph system with a radioactive substance that can then be x-rayed to determine the extent of swelling in the system.

I was injected with a green dye in six doses, three in each foot —right in the webbing between the toes. I had never before thought about how sensitive that area is. After an hour, the dye had penetrated the area well enough to proceed.

Two young Navy doctors appeared, and after I had been given a local anesthetic they each took one foot and began to cut into the top of it. The objective was to find the tiny lymph nodes in the feet and then inject the radioactive substance into them by means of apparatus much like an ordinary intravenous system.

The trick is finding the lymph nodes. The doctors labored away with their special glasses and surgical equipment. It did not go particularly well.

Finally, the lymph node in one foot was located, and I was hooked up to the intravenous system. In time the other was found in the second incision and that foot was connected as well. The flow of the radioactive substance was painful, and I was given a shot of Demerol. As a result, for the latter part of the five-hour procedure, I was floating under the effects of the drug. Increasingly and blissfully oblivious to anything but a sense of removal and quietude, I roamed through an unending series of thoughts. The comfortable unreality was pleasurable, and I understood for the first time why people escape into drugs and alcohol. Even under its alluring effects, I felt intermittent waves of conviction, conviction that I had to get the best of this situation.

Dr. Veach was concerned about the length of time the procedure was taking. We talked briefly, and he seemed to relate to me as a person, not as a senator. The discussion was medical, but not clinical. As he left, he held my shoulder in a gesture of support. I was genuinely moved. I would not see him again, and those brief five minutes would reduce the resentment I felt, fairly or unfairly, about Bethesda.

When it was over, I put my shoes on over my swollen feet, and they just barely fit. The choice was simple—walk comfortably in stocking feet out of the hospital to the car or walk painfully in shoes out of the hospital to the car. Senators do not walk around in public places in their stocking feet. So out I hobbled, painful step after painful step, looking as derelict and undignified and unsenatorial as one can imagine. By the time I reached the hospital garage, I cursed my stupidity, took off my shoes, and stepped in my stocking feet the rest of the way. During these two weeks when it was appropriate to be tough, I had not been; and when it was inappropriate to be tough, I had been.

I drove home and parked in front of our house. The children were inside, so I had to put on my shoes. They had never seen their father coming home from work shoeless. As soon as I had limped upstairs, I took off the shoes and put on my running shoes with the laces untied. The relief was enormous.

"Daddy, your shoelaces are untied."

"Uh, yes. I know."

"Aren't you going to tie them?"

"I don't think so."

"Why not? You're always yelling at us for not having our shoelaces tied."

"Go do your homework."

It was wonderful being home. Except for the x-rays next Tuesday, Bethesda was behind me. I didn't know what was ahead of me, but it was just nice being home.

I spoke with Dennis on the phone. My absence from Massachusetts during a Senate recess had caused increasing comment. In addition to the events of Tuesday and Wednesday, I had canceled Thursday's as well. Two Chamber of Commerce speeches, four hours of fundraising meetings, and a press conference with Governor Mike and Kitty Dukakis on behalf of an art exhibit for Cambodian refugees.

Dennis had been getting calls from people asking what was wrong with me. Flowers arrived at Macomb Street from the Concord Democratic Town Committee wishing me a speedy recovery. Recovery from what? How much did they know? Both the Washington and Boston offices were buzzing. Since Chris Chamberlin was aware of the lump in my groin and knew that the talk of a hernia had never surfaced again, would he put two and two together? What about Marsha Ponte and Chris Naylor, who knew all about my comings and goings to Dr. Cary's office and Bethesda? How long could I go on without being honest with them? But the dilemma was real. Once the forty-four people on my staff were told the truth, the word would spread immediately. Even if each one only informed the individual closest to him or her, the news would expand geometrically. The press was too aggressive in Lowell and Boston and Washington to ignore rumors when they followed a week of mysterious absence. When confronted by a hustling reporter, could my entire staff pretend ignorance convincingly? Not a chance, not everyone. And it would take only one person to expose the whole charade.

Saturday, October 15, 1983

I had to get back on schedule and act normally.

Katina had as usual climbed into bed with us. I was about to walk downstairs when Niki pointed to the bandages on the top of my feet. I diverted Katina's attention and put on my socks. Acting normal would require concentration.

Late that morning I was to speak to the Massachusetts Savings Bank Association's annual convention. These bankers had been very good to me over the years despite my being a Democrat, and a liberal Democrat at that. It was my efforts in favor of

downtown economic development and my support of their legislative agenda that had overcome their natural conservatism.

Doug McGarrah of my staff met me in the hotel lobby with
a look of concern on his face. My slow walk did not reassure him.

"Are you all right?"

"Yeah, I'm fine."

"You know that the Pittsfield people are furious about your
canceling them out again."

"Well, we'll just reschedule it, and they'll get over it."

"I hope so. You've really raised their expectations about helping them on the downtown project, and these cancellations aren't
making any sense to them."

"We'll reschedule it. Now, what the hell has been said to the
bankers so far?"

My friends at the convention greeted me when I entered the
ballroom. I tried to act casual and lighthearted, but I couldn't.
This was my first attempt at normal routine, and it was a lot more
difficult than I had imagined. Basically, I didn't want to be there.
I felt like an intruder—as if this world had gone somewhere,
leaving me behind.

When the time came to speak, I did my usual routine. A little
humor and a lot of substance—that's the prescription. But the
humor was awful and the substance was dull. They had seen and
heard me before, and this was obviously a stumbling performance. At the end they applauded politely and I left. I hoped they
would think I was simply having a bad day.

Doug walked with me to my car.

"Are you sure you're all right?"

"Yes, I'm fine."

But I wasn't fine. If this was normalcy, it wasn't workable. The
sense of alienation from the audience, the sense of otherworldli-
ness, was overwhelming. Rather than being close to a group that
included many longtime supporters and friends, I felt like E.T.
Home, I thought, home.

Niki and I did some errands while I described the session with the bankers. She was pleased that I was going to Boston that evening to get back on schedule and was not going to let a single episode change my plans. Although I wanted to remain in the comfort of our house and family, it would be giving in to weakness. Again I was struck by her strength. "Get up there and get back to normal. We'll miss you, but we'll be okay."

What goes through the mind of a thirty-seven-year-old woman with three small children when all of a sudden her husband gets cancer?

A sense of grief, a sense of anger, a sense of loss, a sense of fear? In what combination? How often does she contemplate what she will do if her husband dies? Does she feel abandoned by him? Does she regret having postponed her career? These questions would haunt me.

I would regularly complain about Niki's leaving the top off the tube of toothpaste, about losing track of her checking account, about discarding coffee cups in my car, about leaving lights on unnecessarily. Did I really spend time on such foolish peeves? How could I be so petty? What about the future? Would our marriage survive all this strain? Yes, I had no doubt about that. Whatever I had to face, I would not be alone. I vowed to spend the effort to really appreciate what that meant. To hell with toothpaste tops.

I arrived in Boston around 6:00. The farther I got from Niki and the kids, the more difficult would be the task—that was obvious. Home was like an emotional space capsule, and you could only go so far away from it before you needed to get back. I would be away until late the next night. I felt like a child going off to school for the first time.

Toby Dilworth of my staff drove me to Concord and talked about everything but the obvious. We often kidded Toby, grandson of former Philadelphia mayor Richardson Dilworth and Yale graduate, about being our "token Yankee." His personality is gregarious, which serves him well as a political organizer. This night, however, for the first time in my six years with him, he was a prototypical Yankee—discreet and reserved. My absence had been topic number one in the office, but if I didn't mention it, he wouldn't mention it. So we talked about our leafleting efforts during primary day in Boston, the organization of precincts and wards around the state, political scuttlebutt on Beacon Hill.

In Concord the town democratic committee was holding a fundraiser at the home of State Senator Chester and Corey Atkins. Concord has been as strong a base of political and financial support as I have ever had. From county commissioner to congressman to senator, I had always had Concord in my column, so there was a good crowd, most of whom had worked for me or contributed to me over the years.

My arrival surprised some who had been told I was ill. After an exchange of inquiries and reassurances about my health the evening took its normal sociable course.

But here in the midst of long-standing friendship—and in some cases, real affection—I felt alone. In a way this was even more unsettling than the earlier session with the bankers. I had assumed that being among my friends would warm me. But my secret had set me apart and caused me to feel different. If I was this way with friends, how would I do with strangers?

Eventually I got up on a chair in the living room and gave a short talk followed by a question-and-answer session. It was fortunate that the group was supportive, because my performance was poor.

Toby and I drove back to Boston to attend the Italian-American Charitable Society dinner at the Copley Plaza Hotel. The honored guest was John Zamparelli, Middlesex County registrar of deeds and frequent toastmaster at my fundraisers.

Seated at the head table, I came to realize that the alienation I had experienced in Concord was even greater here. A few people in attendance were friends of long standing, including Zamparelli and the Massachusetts attorney general, Frank Bellotti, but many were first-time acquaintances. It would be three hours before the evening was over, and I performed like an automaton. I wanted to leave, but I couldn't. I forced myself to eat, made mindless conversation, and kept urging the organizers to begin the program. Finally after an eternity, I was called upon to speak. I gave a short, poor talk and left before the rest of the program—including a speech by Ted Kennedy—was over.

Walter Foster, a recent Dartmouth graduate on my staff, drove me to Lowell. The ride was quiet. I had been awful, and Walter knew it. No going around the tables shaking hands, poorly delivered remarks, and leaving before Ted Kennedy spoke. He must have wondered whether I realized I was in a campaign. I always believed that my staff was reasonably proud of me, but now I felt a sense of embarrassment.

There were thirteen months till next November. Could I go through with this charade for that long? Things would have to get better. Thirteen months of days like this and I would be a basket case.

The Lowell house was cold and empty when I arrived. Since I went straight to bed, it remained so when I awoke before dawn. I didn't want to be there. I wanted to be in Washington. That time waiting for the sun to come up was spent reflecting upon the previous evening's fiascos. It was one thing being away from Niki and the kids, but it was quite another to be screwing up the campaign in the process.

Again I found myself trying to reach out for a sense of spirituality. Why was it that I called upon God only when things went wrong? Why didn't I reach out in good times? He certainly owed me nothing, given my neglect of expressing my gratitude for previous gifts.

Sunday, October 16, 1983

Nick Rizzo drove me to Milton for a Temple Shalom breakfast. Being with Nick made me feel better. His older-brother attitude was welcome.

We talked about my health and how people would react to the news of the cancer. Nick was sure that people would be sympathetic and it would be difficult for anyone to run against me. I was not so certain. But only by telling the truth would we find out.

We drove down Route 3 to Route 128. "I'm going to tell you something, and I don't want you to say anything," he said.

"What is it?"

"Promise me you won't say anything."

"Nick, stop playing games. If you have something to say, say it."

"You and I talked about your economic future when you were in the hospital."

"So?"

"And we talked about your being associated with some local corporations if you left the Senate. Right?"

"Yes?"

"And you thought it would be a good idea."

"Yes, I remember."

"During this week I contacted Paul Guzzi at Wang Labs, Jim Dineen at Raytheon, and Jack Sampson at Bay State Gas."

"So?"

"Well, they've all agreed to hire you as a consultant to their companies in 1985 if you are defeated for reelection."

"Nick, you're kidding."

"No, I'm not kidding. I told them I was trying to get a handle on your 1985 plans just in case you lost."

"You didn't?"

"I did."

"Do they think I sent you to them?" I screamed.

"Paul, shut up. I told them I was doing this on my own, that you knew nothing about it."

"Nick, who the hell's going to believe that?"

The thought of these people being approached horrified me. It was like asking for a handout. Besides, I was an incumbent United States senator. They might think I sent Nick to ask for a damn job if I lost a race no one believed I could lose.

I would have to get in touch with them and straighten it out. I realized that they would not have made any commitments, given the companies involved, but they must have been shocked. I had to speak to them before they talked to too many people about my apparent heavy-handedness. I turned to Nick to demand that he call them as well, but the anguish over my newly tarnished reputation quickly evaporated. Looking at Nick's hurt reaction to my response, I realized that here was a good friend trying to protect me and my family. Besides, he had really thought I wanted him to do it.

From anger I was soon moved to immense gratitude.

"You stupid bastard," I said, "you don't go around doing things like that."

"If you're so smart, how come you've got cancer and your family isn't provided for in case you're incapacitated? Huh? Answer me that!"

"But Nick, you don't . . ."

"Look, Senator, you've had a good time being a whoopie liberal, traveling around this country and the world, speaking to other whoopie liberals. Meanwhile your net worth is an embarrassment, and who gets hurt? Not you. Your family. I've been telling you to save some money all these years, but, no, you wouldn't listen. Now you've got your rear end in a bind and you're mad at me. You ought to be mad at yourself."

We were silent for a few moments.

Nick filled the air in the car with cigarette smoke and it bothered me, but I left the window closed.

"Nick, for a fascist, you're a good friend."

"I know."

"And if you had any brains, you wouldn't smoke."

"You're the one with cancer, whoopie."

We laughed, and I opened the window to let in the fresh air. I had never had an older brother, but Nick was a reasonably good substitute.

Some day Guzzi and Dineen and Sampson would understand. I decided not to call them, but made Nick promise not to do anything else.

The day was sunny, and I thought about asking Nick to drive on; we could forget my appearance in Milton and do something together.

"I don't feel like giving a speech on the Middle East," I said.

"Good. I don't feel like hearing you give a speech, so I'm going to drop you off there and go home and watch the football games."

In Milton, Lawry Payne of my staff met us at the parking lot of the temple. We were late, and he was concerned. The congregation was waiting for me, so after a quick swing through the kitchen to say hello to the volunteers who had prepared the breakfast, I joined the group.

The introduction by the master of ceremonies was gracious. He said that they had heard I was ill and might have to cancel my appearance. However, I had gotten better and was there, and "we thank God for returning you to good health."

If only it were true.

I looked down at Lawry and saw he was studying me. We had traveled to the Middle East together, and after five years on my staff he knew me very well. Now he wanted to see how I reacted to the statement about my health.

I just smiled. Here I was being scrutinized by Lawry, who would see great significance in every nuance. Obviously my earlier absence had not gone unnoticed by my Boston staff. They all knew something was happening, but what? Somebody had to find out. It was Lawry's turn to play detective. Usually my staff wasn't anxious to hear me speak on a subject they had heard me on before. As my Massachusetts expert on the Middle East, Lawry had listened to me often on the subject and knew every detail of my position. He should have been dozing in his chair. He wasn't. He watched me like a trainer looking at a horse rumored to have a bad ankle.

The audience was a new one for me, and it listened carefully to my discourse about events in the Middle East—Israel, Lebanon, and the Iran-Iraq war. Questions followed, and I was very much at ease. At the end of the talk, a woman came up to me and said, "I never realized you had such a good sense of humor."

Walking out, Lawry said, "You did well."

I thought the speech had been average—not great, but not a disaster either, like the previous night's. Like Toby Dilworth, Lawry would not inquire, but I could sense his anxiety.

He drove me to Brookline to my sister's house. I had two hours of free time, since Sunday noon is hard to schedule, and Thaleia's house was convenient.

Thaleia, Vicki, and Vicki's husband, Jim, were in the kitchen. It was the first time I had seen Vicki and Jim since I had discovered the lump.

We hugged each other and allowed the tears to flow. This had not happened since our father had died two years before. The re-creation of that scene made me remember him, and the moment seemed all the more poignant, the mixture of past pain with future fear.

There was almost a sense of fatalism. I felt as if I were being mourned, and I mourned as well.

The emotional tide crested and ebbed quickly. We could now

talk about "it" and soon were able to speak about other matters. An hour later I was listening to the Patriots game on the radio.

By 1:30 I was back on the road, returning to Milton for the wake of my friend and former House colleague James Burke. As I knelt by his casket to say my prayers, I had a strange sense of calm. Looking at the face of death was less fearful than imagining it. Here death was real, yet somehow contained and with some order. Jimmy had died, but he had lived a long, productive life.

The inevitable crossed my mind. Would this tableau be repeated for me? And when? I prayed for Jimmy Burke, but I also prayed for Paul Tsongas. I prayed for time. Time to let my family grow up.

As I walked back to the car, I was almost detached from my dilemma. Death comes to everyone. The only question is when.

The rest of the day was more normal and thus strangely harder. I attended a fundraiser on my behalf in Hingham, and gave a speech to the International Hand Surgeons Convention in Boston.

By 7:25 I was on the plane returning to Washington. The weekend was over. I had been in six different political situations, and while I had not done very well, I had, on balance, not done very badly either. I had functioned. Reflecting on it, I decided that twelve and a half months of this kind of existence would make for a very, very long campaign. Away from home every weekend as well as some weekdays. An empty house in Lowell until June. After that, weekdays in Washington in a different empty house, since Niki and the children would have moved to Lowell. The twelve and a half months seemed an eternity. And if I won—six more years of it. Some prize.

But it had to be. The fight was mental as well as physical. And I could climb out of this psychic valley of darkness only if I was doing something I enjoyed and that had meaning to me. Since I loved the Senate and it clearly had meaning, it was a necessary part of my rehabilitation. The alternative was to crawl back to

Lowell like a wounded, pathetic creature. That I would not do. While I was deep in the valley at this point, leaving the Senate would drive me to its very depths. Staying in the Senate was my ticket to emotional health, and I was grateful that this option existed. I was especially grateful that I didn't have what seemed to be a difficult campaign.

Again, arriving home was a joy. The children normally would be in bed by 8:00, but it was past 9:00 when I drove up to the house. Niki had kept them up and had orchestrated a fond welcome when I opened the door. It was corny and overplayed and just great.

That night I reported everything to Niki like a child coming back from camp. I did this, I did that. I saw this, I saw that. When I told her about Nick's serving as my employment agency, she reacted the same way I did—shock and then laughter.

I also asked her about church. It was Sunday night, and since I had been away all day in Massachusetts, I had not gone to St. Alban's. I missed the experience. And missing it surprised me. I thought about that a lot.

Monday, October 17, 1983

After walking the children to school, I drove in to work. The everydayness of driving in satisfied me.

I pulled up to the curb in front of the Russell Building and said hello to the Capitol police officers on the street and those at the security checkpoint inside the door.

"Good morning, Senator."

This was the way it had been for almost five years. This building, these people, this job—it was going to be as before. I took the elevator to the third floor and began the walk down the long marbled corridor past the various Senate offices. Several staffers passed me and gave me a cheery good morning.

By the time I reached the end of the corridor, I had gone from pleasure in the normal routine to the realization that I was fooling myself. Things were not normal. They would never be normal again. I had cancer, and that was not normal, nor was it going to change. It was there, and pretending otherwise in flights of avoidance would eventually cause me to crash to earth. Cancer could not be cured by routines. It had to be faced up to. It had to be fought. It could not be wished away.

I sat down at my desk and tried to go through the paperwork that had accumulated during the Senate recess. My heart wasn't in it, and I found myself reading letters or memos over and over and not comprehending the words. I had a serious agenda to contemplate, and this routine of Senate business was not it.

I finally gave up and went to the gym. This was becoming a habit.

The routine there *was* normal. Exercise was a lift to my spirits. It reaffirmed my physical capacities and gave me something to push against. One of the attendants noticed the bandages on my feet and asked what had happened. I explained that it was from wearing new running shoes; they had chafed my skin. (I had used the same excuse earlier that morning when Katina had seen my feet before I could get my socks on.)

Back to the office and more paperwork. Since it was the first day in session after the recess, little was happening. Many members were still traveling to Washington, so nothing important would take place so as not to inconvenience those who had to come from the distant states.

Marsha interrupted to say that Bethesda had called, and I had an appointment there tomorrow morning. (This would be to take the x-rays to measure the results of the angiogram procedure.) I thanked her and tried to concentrate on the papers on my desk.

A little later, I looked up and found Marsha and Chris Naylor coming in and closing the door behind them. They sat down in front of my desk.

"Okay," Chris said. "What's going on?"

Some normalcy.

"What do you mean?" I said weakly.

"Paul, don't kid us. Dr. Cary, Bethesda, the week in Massachusetts canceled, and now back to Bethesda tomorrow. And all without any explanation. We want to know what's happening. Are you all right?"

Senators do not get confronted by their staffs. I never did. My staff has free access to me, and almost everyone eventually feels comfortable enough about coming in and raising issues, concerns, or disagreements.

This was different. What struck me was not their obvious concern. What struck me was the totally stern, businesslike nature of their conduct. It was like a mutiny. A reversal of roles.

I didn't want to tell anyone else just yet. So far the circle of awareness had included my family members, Dennis, Rich, and Nick. That was it. It would not—and could not—expand further. Once more and more people knew, the word would get out, and not on the terms that I could control. It was critical that I determine the content and timing of any announcement of my illness.

I was about to say that nothing was wrong, and they should forget it. But instead I paused and realized how futile that would be. Chris again broke the silence.

"Paul, we know that something is going on, and we want to know what it is."

"Well," I said, "I've got a problem. And I've been having tests to see what it's all about. The tests aren't complete yet—that's why I'm going back to Bethesda tomorrow. I wasn't going to say anything, but when the tests are done, I'll tell you what's happening. You'll have to bear with me for a while. What have you been saying to people about last week?"

"Nothing. Dennis said you weren't feeling well, and that's what we've said. No one knows about Bethesda. Everyone's asking questions, but we've said nothing about Bethesda, because it would cause real concern."

"No one knows about Bethesda?"

"No one, not even our husbands. We didn't feel it was our prerogative to say anything."

These were not mutineers. This was the Praetorian Guard.

It was time to be a bit more frank.

"What I have is serious, but we don't know how serious. The tests will tell the story. Could you get Dr. Canellos on the phone so I can arrange to meet with him and have everything analyzed?"

They left, and I felt very grateful. Their display of discretion and loyalty was moving. No rumors, no cashing in on "inside" information.

I went into Dennis's office and told him that I had confided in Marsha and Chris. He agreed that it made sense. So the circle of awareness expanded by two; it would not grow again for three months.

When Dr. Canellos called back, I suggested Friday morning for an appointment, since I had a speech in Boston that day. That way it would not arouse any undue interest.

He disagreed.

"Come on Saturday. The institute is closed, and no one will be around. We'll meet in my office. I'll take a look at you, and we can talk without any time constraints and without anyone knowing you were here. I'll meet you in the lobby at eleven."

We agreed on the time and that I would arrange to get the test results from Bethesda up to him by Thursday. Dennis was going to Boston anyway, so he would carry the test results and meet Thaleia at the airport, and she could leave them at the doctor's office.

I felt like a cocaine smuggler. Secret transfer of vital information. Clandestine meetings.

Tuesday, October 18, 1983

Tuesday I went to Bethesda to finish up the tests. Driving out there reignited all the old fears, but knowing that this was the end mitigated them.

The tests were completed quickly, and arrangements were made for Dennis to pick up the results the next morning.

Driving away from Bethesda for the last time down Wisconsin Avenue, I was struck with a sense of enormous release. I arrived at the Capitol in time to attend the latter half of the Democratic Senators' Tuesday lunch. I felt almost light-headed. I sat down next to Pat Moynihan of New York at the most distant table so as not to disrupt the proceedings. After almost three weeks of emotional blowout, I had been scarcely eating at all, having lost my appetite completely and about ten pounds in the process. (This did not help my morale, since weight loss is a sign of the lymphoma's becoming aggressive, and I couldn't tell whether it was the stress or the lymphoma that was to blame.) At the lunch I absolutely devoured the food in front of me—including four desserts. My relief at putting Bethesda behind me released my suppressed appetite. For me, it was a memorable feast. As someone who is somewhat careful about diet, I often feel guilty about dessert at lunch, and here I was eating *four* and seeing it almost as a sacred duty in order to get my weight back up. It was the first time in years that I had gorged myself totally free of remorse. I tried not to have my colleagues notice this alarming display of self-indulgence. Fortunately, the minority leader, Senator Robert Byrd, was showing TV tapes of commercials that had been used in the various 1982 campaigns, and so the room was darkened. Rolls, salad, lunch, and two trips to the food table for double desserts, all by the flickering light of the TV. If anyone noticed, he was kind enough to keep it to himself.

Wednesday, October 19, 1983

Solar-lobby press conference, Worcester Jewish Community luncheon, Anti-Defamation League luncheon, newspaper interview on presidential race, reception for winners of National Science Foundation Presidential Awards, meeting Foreign Minister D'Escoto of Nicaragua with the Foreign Relations Committee.

The routine, however, was broken by Rich and Dennis. I was in Room 189 of the Russell Office Building waiting for the ADL meeting to proceed when they called me into the corridor outside.

Thaleia had phoned them earlier to relate a conversation with Dr. Canellos. The discussion was optimistic, and she said that the average expectancy was not eight years but twelve years and likely even more. They wanted to get this good news to me right away.

I exploded in anger.

The uplift of the day before had dissolved into a quiet sense of dread about the Saturday meeting with Canellos. There we would get the final answers, and the anticipation of such finality had a brooding dimension to it. Now Thaleia was calling with her amateur prognosis and juicing up the roller coaster even more. I didn't want to hear it. I didn't want to grab at straws that could not be sustained. "No, I will not call her back," I said and abruptly walked back into the room.

My anger surprised all of us, and I realized the shallowness of my veneer of normalcy.

Friday, October 21, 1983

Friday I flew up to Boston for a speech to the Food Marketing Institute, then returned to Washington to meet with interior secretary nominee Judge William Clark and attend a reception for Dennis Brutus, the exiled black South African poet. All my thoughts were on 11:00 at the Dana-Farber Cancer Institute the next day.

Niki and I decided to spend Saturday night on Cape Cod with her parents. Whatever the analysis was, it made no sense to go back right away to Washington. So we arranged for Suzi Sauvage, one of Niki's sisters, to stay with the children, and I told Chris to cancel my appearance Saturday afternoon at a conference on neoliberalism conducted by Charles Peters of *The Washington Monthly*. I couldn't have returned in time anyway. Trying to give the appearance of normalcy was one thing, but rigid adherence to the schedule on such a day was too much.

Saturday, October 22, 1983

Both Niki and I woke up before dawn on Saturday. The children raced downstairs to watch Saturday-morning cartoons. By 9:35 they had a baby-sitter, and we were on the plane to Boston.

We didn't know how to feel. The answers were in Canellos's office and we were going there. Flying to Boston to have someone tell us what was going on in my body, which was on the plane. The cancer had moved to Dana-Farber. It was on the x-rays and angiogram and CAT-scan printouts and blood tests. And we were going to Boston to be reunited with it.

How strange.

David Goldman of my staff met us at Logan. He had been told that we were going to the Cape to see my in-laws. He gave me the keys to the campaign car. I was about to get into it when I noticed that it had a Tsongas-for-Senate sticker on it. That would not do. There was no way to sneak into Dana-Farber incognito when I had the damn sticker proclaiming my presence to everyone who saw the car. My paranoia was running wild. I began to try to pull it off, but it was sealed onto the back window.

David was staring at me. Why would I be doing that?

Niki had her wits about her, fortunately, and told me we had to go. So off we went, leaving David with his thoughts.

It was a beautiful New England fall day. October 22, 1983. Twenty-four days from the "hernia." Twenty-four days of mostly hell—and all roller coaster. The toughest period of my life by far. The "first day of the rest of my life." I had never liked that all-too-cute saying, but it certainly applied here.

We drove over to the Brookline Avenue complex of medical excellence. Beth Israel, where Ashley and Molly had been born, Children's Hospital, Harvard University Medical School, and the Dana-Farber Cancer Institute. We found the right side street because of the sign, "Dana-Farber Cancer Institute." I had often been on that street before and had never noticed the sign. Now it loomed large and imposing. Particularly the word "cancer."

We parked illegally in a partly empty lot and entered the institute. The lobby was empty, with only a guard at the reception desk. I approached him and said we were to meet Dr. Canellos.

"Oh yes. Dr. Canellos said he was going to meet someone here. He's in already. Why don't you sit over there. He'll be back shortly."

I thanked the guard and wondered whether he recognized me with my glasses on. Given the weight on my heart, it was a small concern. Niki and I wandered over to the glass-enclosed gift shop to peer into the windows. There were no sounds, no one moving around.

After a few minutes a voice said, "Senator Tsongas?" I turned around, and we met Dr. Canellos for the first time. He was tallish, in his late forties, with horn-rimmed glasses. But he was dressed in a blue double-breasted blazer with gray slacks. No white doctor's coat. He looked as if he were on his way to a yacht club for cocktails. Consistent with that, his demeanor was cheerful, casual, and not the least troubled.

We small-talked about time and weather and parking as we took the elevator up to the top floor, where his office was. The entire floor was deserted, and we followed him into his office with its sweeping view southwest to some small hills with their fall foliage ablaze.

"So, how are you feeling?" Canellos's question and manner remained light and almost floating. His tone was as if he knew me well and had asked me if the Bruins had won the night before. A little closer to home than my question about Israel.

"Fine," I lied. I was not fine. I was damn scared, and my voice betrayed my attempt at nonchalance.

I was no longer the senator from Massachusetts. I was a frightened human being who loved his wife and children, and desperately wanted to live. And we were here, seated around this wood-grained table, to find out if I would—and if I would, how long.

"I got all the tests from Bethesda. They certainly did a very thorough job. Even the angiogram. We hardly ever do that anymore here, but having it as well is fine." He pointed to the top of his bookshelves, where a stack of x-ray covers and other material had been placed. "That's you up there."

I looked up at the files that had journeyed there from Bethesda clandestinely. I was up there and yet I was right here. Those files and materials were informing him what was inside of me.

"Now, let me tell you what the story is," he said. His words were serious and businesslike, but his voice wasn't. There was no touch of trauma or dread or pity or morbidity.

He leaned back in his chair and began the long exposition.

It was lymphoma, a cancer. Of the various kinds of cancer, it was quite treatable, especially the type of lymphoma I had.

There were many kinds of cancer and many kinds of noncancer illnesses that were a lot worse. This lymphoma had not been cured before, although there were rare instances of unexplained total remissions. But there had been a great deal of medical research in the past few years, and the body of knowledge was growing rapidly. Many people had the disease and lived for years completely without treatment. When and if it became aggressive, I would get some chemotherapy to knock it back down. It would not cure me, but the chances were very good that it would work. And the chemotherapy would not be debilitating.

The tests from Bethesda showed that, contrary to the preliminary analysis of Dr. Shen, the lymphoma had spread to my bone marrow, but only in very small quantities. And that was to be expected. So the choice of treatment was to either reduce the swollen lymph nodes or have no treatment. Since the lymph nodes in my armpits and neck and shoulder were small, there was no reason to be treated at this time. And indeed, it might be years before treatment would be necessary. Canellos went on to tell us about a doctor who had the same illness and had not been treated for three years and jogged every day and was doing just fine. He would arrange for me to meet him someday.

He spoke about some current experiments in treatment. One involved taking a lymph node and extracting the cells to make antibodies—I had been told about that at Bethesda. I had been scheduled to become a guinea pig for that research, and he affirmed that it was worth trying. The other consisted of the removal of bone marrow, cleansing it of the cancerous cells, and freezing it for later use during chemotherapy. This reintroduction of clean bone marrow would allow the body to withstand more toxic doses of chemotherapy.

Canellos went on to describe the cancer, how it probably had begun several years ago and had not manifested itself until the lump appeared in my groin.

On and on we went, back and forth. It was part great detail and part great hope.

"What about life expectancy? What about the eight-year figure?"

Eight years was only a statistical average, and indeed the more recent data would suggest twelve or more (Thaleia had been right after all). But the average was meaningless in individual cases. At what point did the clock on the eight or twelve years begin to run? When a lump first appeared, or when the patient first sought out a doctor? Besides, such a measure doesn't take into account ongoing research and discovery.

We absorbed the data and the hope.

. "Well, what do you think I should say when I announce that I have this?"

He looked at me with great seriousness and surprise.

"I wouldn't announce it."

"But I have to. I think people have a right to know about such a thing in a campaign."

"Why?" Now the easy manner was gone.

"Because I've always been open about my finances, my tax returns."

He looked at me with a faint scowl.

"We're not talking about your tax returns. The public has a right to know about the lymphoma when and if it begins to affect you or when you are receiving treatment. Even then we could argue the case for silence, but certainly nothing should be revealed before then. People look at cancer as if it were some medieval disease and just can't deal with it. You will not be treated normally, because they can't get over the societal prejudice."

He went on to describe his anger about the ignorance surrounding cancer. No capacity to differentiate between variations of the disease. No knowledge about cure rates or effective treatment.

He had decided to work in oncology because he had confidence that cancer could be fought. He pointed out that the institute was not the Dana-Farber Institute, it was the Dana-Farber *Cancer* Institute. They were not about to run away from that word.

Canellos related stories about people who learned that they had cancer and began the process of dying instead of living. People who were determined to fight back had done so successfully. I felt awful. During the past twenty-four days I had been much nearer the former category. I was ashamed.

He then came back to the question of public disclosure.

"And what about your children?" he persisted. "Are you going to tell them? If you announce it, you'll have to. Is it fair to them when you probably will be all right for a long time? Why put this kind of burden on them at their age for no valid reason?"

I fell silent. Niki agreed with him. Finally, I said I would think about it. I had always assumed that it would be disclosed once we knew exactly what it was. The idea of hiding it for months during a campaign—indeed, potentially for years—was unsettling. But his arguments had found their mark and when they were reinforced by Niki, the issue had been decided in favor of secrecy even though I didn't know it at the time.

Canellos was like an old family friend as we talked about the future. I looked up to the top of the bookshelves at my files and they no longer frightened me. I then gazed out at the lovely fall day and found I was indeed thinking about the years ahead.

It had been two and a half hours when he escorted us down the elevator and back through the still-deserted lobby.

"Keep in touch, and if you need me, call. Go to Dr. Ihde every two months or so, and I'll see you after you've moved back. You're in better physical shape than I am, so keep it up and enjoy your children."

The jury had come in with its verdict. Guilty, all right, but the sentence would be light. The prisoner is released into probation and will be observed.

We thanked him, retrieved the car, and headed for Cape Cod. Niki looked over at me and managed to avoid saying "I told you so."

She had been right all along. Right about being optimistic and right about the value of sharing all of this together. It had been a hellish twenty-four days, but probably the closest twenty-four of our fourteen years together. We had learned a great deal about a lot of things—including each other.

What about the future? It was only 1:00. There would be time to see a real estate agent in Harwich and look at property before we were due at Meme and Opa's (our children's names for my in-laws).

A house on the Cape.

The future.

Our hearts sang all the way down the highway.

Chapter 5

The Decision

Cape Cod is a lovely quirk of nature. Extending out into the Atlantic and warmed by the Gulf Stream, it offers a charm that one does not find easily on our crowded eastern seaboard.

For me it holds pleasant memories of summers spent teaching swimming while in college and law school, of my children learning to swim at the Wychmere Harbor Club in Harwich—and of October 22, 1983.

After the psychic emancipation in Dr. Canellos's office, the drive to the Cape was filled with the simple wonder of life. I was able to see what I was looking at with a mind prepared to contemplate it.

Sun, clouds, marshes, the North River, the Cape Cod Canal, Barnstable Harbor—I saw what I had seen hundreds of times before but not in the same way. I don't mean to overstate the case and it's hard to draw the distinction accurately, but there is a distinction.

Walking from the Russell Senate Office Building to the Capitol to vote has been a normal everyday occurrence in my work life—unless, of course, it's raining hard or very cold. I have always taken that seven-minute walk with my head down lost in thought or conversation. It has been a time to ponder, to calculate, to absorb data, to plan—to do anything but look up and notice whether the trees were budding or even what kind of trees were there.

How often I had driven to Cape Cod thinking about whatever and not noticing what nature had created along the way—intent upon how long it was taking or how many miles remained of the trip.

Not so on October 22, 1983. To Niki and me, everything was more wondrous, and we drew deep satisfaction from what had been given to us.

We spent two hours looking at property in Harwich. We had estimated the profit from selling our house in Washington and were anxious to convert that sum into a Cape Cod summer home. It would be the first step of a new arrangement. But the fall real estate pickings were slim, and nothing appealed.

By 5:00 P.M., we arrived at Meme and Opa's house to have dinner, talk, and enjoy each other's company. My mother-in-law had just left the hospital after a severe bout with an unknown virus. She was much better, and I was much better, and so the evening went well.

Sunday, October 23, 1983

We read the Sunday papers and just loafed. By late morning, however, we were retracing our steps to Boston. Niki had to get back to Washington, and I took her to Logan Airport. I would stay in Lowell, since I was scheduled to give a speech early the next morning in Cambridge. It was a sign of my emotional calm that I could think of not returning to D.C. It made no logistical sense, and there was no point in trying to eke out every moment with the family, only to turn around the next morning and return to Boston.

I took Niki to the plane and watched it leave the gate. Whatever else I had done in my life, I had certainly married well. But I never knew how very well until the "hernia" appeared. Niki could be a tough battler in ways that her gentleness did not suggest.

I drove to Lowell and spent the afternoon watching the football games and trying to cook caches of food from the freezer. Evening came and I shuttled between the television set, the refrigerator, and a hot bathtub.

The days that followed are not clear memories for me. Much of the trauma had passed, and with it there was a lessening of the intensity of each day and each event. I look over my schedules and notes, but the details are only dimly etched in my mind.

The last week of October was spent voting on issues like the federal budget and the MX and making speeches in several different places. It was a week like all of my political weeks—nothing out of the ordinary.

Ordinary. How fortunate I was to have my days filled with the great issues of our time. One after another. And how accustomed I was to concentrate on arms control one week, high-technology innovation the next week, human rights in El Salvador the week after that.

What I distinctly remember about that October work week and the three that followed was that my fear of and concern about the lymphoma had virtually passed. It seemed a matter for the future—the long-term future. I would worry about it then. Sometimes at the end of a day I would realize that I had not thought about the lymphoma for hours on end, in contrast to the total concentration before the Canellos meeting.

I am not sure whether I had removed it from my mind or had actually come to grips with it. Whatever the explanation, the weeks went on with a sense of calm. It was a calm, however, that seemed characterless, lacking in true appreciation of how wonderful every day of life really is.

As November proceeded along, my focus returned to the campaign. I had worked hard for five years, and that work had apparently scared off any primary competition. There were people who wouldn't hesitate to run against me if they thought they could win. I don't say that critically. It's a fact of life, just as I did not hesitate for long to contest Senator Edward Brooke despite having few, if any, differences on substantive issues. Ours is a truly Darwinian profession.

The fundraising situation, however, was in bad shape. A year before the election we had no finance council in working order, fundraising events were few and far between, and our war chest accumulated over the five years of incumbency was only $60,000. The polls were good and the organization was excellent, but the finances were in disarray. Almost all of my efforts outside of Senate activities were aimed at trying to improve this situation.

The Senate adjourned on November 18 for two months. This was unprecedented in the first year of a legislative session, but it was welcome. I would be able to campaign extensively without missing roll-call votes. It was a convenient situation for an incumbent.

This was my seventh campaign and might be one of the easiest. But there was one nagging worry. Ray Shamie, my likely Republican opponent, was a multimillionaire and was prepared to spend his own money in large quantities. Add that to the funds made available to any Republican by the party Campaign Committee, and I might well be outspent.

But would that make a difference?

I didn't know Shamie; I had merely shaken his hand once during his contest with Ted Kennedy two years before. He seemed a good enough man but was very conservative. Kennedy's staff had given us their "book" on Shamie, and it was quite interesting. It would save us a lot of research and would give us ammunition if we decided to go on the attack.

What if he spent $3 million on a negative campaign? How

much damage could he do? He'd clearly need to cut me up to have any chance at all. My favorable/unfavorable ratio had been in the low 70s/high 60s to mid-teens/low 20s for five years. If those numbers weren't changed, he could never hope to win.

But I didn't believe Shamie was going to be a threat. If he chopped 20 points off the lowest lead I had, my cushion would still be 25 points. If he ever got closer, I could go after him on the issue of his being too doctrinaire a conservative.

It would be more serious were there a strong Democratic challenger followed by a different, more moderate Republican. For example, if the attorney general, Frank Bellotti, took me on, it would be a hard race. If an Elliot Richardson or a Margaret Heckler or an Andrew Card was the Republican after that, it could become very competitive. I believed I could win, but the margins would be much slimmer. Not as tough a fight as 1972, my first race for the Congress, or 1978, the Senate election, but no cakewalk either.

I went to Frederick, Maryland, to the National Cancer Institute on November 1. I was to have another biopsy; this time a lymph node would be removed in order to use it for the experimental antibody research. An hour was spent explaining the theory and procedure to me. Then Dr. Kenneth Foon examined me to determine which lymph node would be removed. He probed and probed, but couldn't find one big enough. The operation was canceled. They weren't big enough—wonderful. I drove back to Washington on a high.

After that, cancer, lymphoma, bone marrow, lymph nodes— all were shelved for future reference. The campaign and how to finance it became my priority. I was back to my normal activities —and my normal perspective. Occasionally I would have an uneasy sense that the lessons I had learned during my worst days were being disregarded now that it was business as usual. But even that sense was ignored.

I was again Paul Tsongas, the United States senator with an

aggressive and ambitious political agenda. November 5 came and went, and I had one year to election night.

Running against an incumbent was what I did best. You take the fight to him. Running as an incumbent is miserable. All you can do is fend off attacks. As the old political expression goes, "It's easier to throw than to catch."

In addition, the physical drain would be dreadful. It would mean days and weeks spent away from home, running around the state. Worse still on an intellectual level, it would mean a great deal of time spent away from issues and substance and instead on fundraising and handholding. Some politicians love campaigns. Most do not. Perhaps there are senators and congressmen who look forward to reelection campaigns, but I never met one.

In mid-November I noticed a discomfort in the back of my neck. I didn't pay any attention to it at first, but by the second day I knew it was not normal. I hardly ever get headaches or other such pains, and this was unprecedented. It had to be a swelling lymph node.

I was back to reality after weeks of paying little attention to "it." In the post-Canellos period, my concern was there but not dominating. I told no one except Niki and saw no reason to inform Canellos. I didn't want to run to him every time I felt a twinge or pain. But it did destroy the illusion that the lymphoma could be kept on a back burner for many years. The swelling in the groin was not an isolated event after all.

By the third day the pain had subsided, but on November 19 I became aware of another area of discomfort in the back of my neck behind the throat. Like the previous one, it could not be felt or seen from the outside. Again I would wait it out and it would also subside.

On November 2c I had an early-morning meeting in the Sheraton Boston Hotel with the Massachusetts Teachers Association. I was seeking their endorsement and was sure to get it, so the session was really a formality. Everything was cordial and substantive. But afterward, I could again sense the discomfort in the back of my throat. I then went to a business/education conference which I was sponsoring with the Massachusetts Business Roundtable and the New England Council. I participated all day except for a brief period away from the conference welcoming Tonsai, the Thai cook who had cared for the Americans during the hostage crisis in Iran. We had helped get his family to America and they were arriving on that day.

By 5:00 I had returned to the conference and the swelling had become more severe. I had a rest period in the hotel before going to a Brookline fundraiser that evening, where Niki would join me.

I sent the staff away, saying I wanted to nap. But I couldn't sleep or even lie down comfortably. I had a sense of being choked.

I thought I'd give this one a chance to go away as the other one had. Lymph nodes are known to swell and recede.

But it only got worse. An hour later I picked up the phone and asked information for the number of the Dana-Farber Institute. Swelling in my groin was one thing. So was pain in my neck. But choking was altogether different.

Dr. Canellos's secretary said he had left but gave me his home number. I called him there, but he wasn't home yet, so I left my number at the hotel.

For the next half-hour I pondered a strategy. I didn't want to take chemotherapy until I absolutely had to. "Let's keep our powder dry," Canellos had advised. But he also said he could give me just enough chemotherapy to reduce any troublesome problem. I kept thinking about his story of the Boston doctor with the same illness who for over two years had refused treatment despite swelling that was visible. He was into his third year and here I was, bailing out after one month.

The phone jarred me out of my thoughts.

"Well, Paul, how are you doing?"

"Fine, Doctor, but I've got a problem I wanted to tell you about. I have a swelling in the back of my throat, and it's bothersome."

"Does it affect your swallowing?"

"Yes, a bit."

"Is it painful?"

"Not very, but it is uncomfortable."

"Well, look, if it's still a problem, why don't I see you on Saturday morning the same as before. I'll arrange to be in my office and I'll meet you around ten-thirty. Is that convenient?"

"Yes."

Pause.

"Ah, Doctor, what if it gets worse in the meantime?" (Translated, this meant, "If I'm choking to death late tonight, could I see you sooner?")

"You have my numbers at the office and here at home. If you need me, just call and I'll see you."

"Okay, thanks. Good night."

I hung up fully expecting to phone him again in a short while. Ten minutes later, my staff came by to get me. Not much choice but to act normal, so off we went to the fundraiser.

At the dinner, everything I ate got caught in my throat just enough to remind me that there was more on my mind than the reelection. The swelling seemed to have stabilized. It wasn't any better, but it wasn't any worse either.

Niki and I returned home to Lowell—it was the Thanksgiving vacation. I went to bed totally concentrated on the lymph node behind my throat, invisible to the eye but all too visible in my mind.

By morning it had receded enough to be appreciably less uncomfortable. It was there, but not enough to drive me to the phone. For the next three days it remained about the same.

On Thanksgiving Day we had a full house. My uncle and aunt from Canada, an Israeli family whom we had visited in their kibbutz apartment a year before, my sisters and their families—

twenty-three people in all. It was a wonderful event, but the shredded carrots kept getting stuck in my throat.

The next day the Kails, former neighbors in Alexandria, flew up to spend the rest of the week. They are close friends—their three children are the same ages as ours. On Friday night, I took Michael Kail on a tour of the development projects in downtown Lowell.

We stopped in the Rex parking lot overlooking the canal locks, and I pointed out where the new Hilton was going to be built. I described the renewal I had helped to bring about. He asked me why we had decided to move the family to Lowell in June.

"Well, because Niki is going back to law school."

"Why can't she go to law school in Washington?"

"It's not as simple as that. There is also the problem of trying to keep both houses now that they've capped our outside honoraria."

"Look, Paul, I know you pretty well after all these years. Is there something else?"

"Yes, there is."

"Is somebody sick?"

"Yes."

"Is it one of Niki's folks?"

"No."

"Is it one of the children?" The deep concern in his voice for our kids moved me.

"No, it's me. I have cancer."

My voice was without emotion. It was as if I had said, "I have a dead battery in my car." For the first time since the Canellos meeting I had told someone about the cancer and could do so without panic or overflowing emotions. I explained it in the context that Canellos had outlined.

"Well, it sounds manageable, from what you say," Michael said after I finished.

"Yes, except for the fact that I have to see the doctor tomorrow because a swelling lymph node is threatening to choke me to death." I meant it humorously, but Michael didn't receive it that way. I would have to be more careful about my jokes. But at least I could joke about it. Fifty-five days had passed since the "hernia," and I still had not been treated. Fifty-five gifts. Each day that passed gave me new strength. Each day put the agonies of October further behind me. This errant lymph node had reinstilled the awareness of mortality, yet the passing days brought a sense of horizon, of perspective. It was an acutely bittersweet combination.

On Saturday I left the two families in Lowell early. The meeting with Canellos was again preceded by our rendezvous in the deserted lobby. He took me into a ground-floor examining room, and we started out talking about presidential politics, ethnic families, and other assorted topics.

A half hour of such conversation passed. This approach baffled me, but it was nice to have him reacting without urgency to my situation.

"So, what's the problem?" he said finally.

I explained how the swelling lymph node had affected my swallowing.

We went into the next room, and he began examining my neck, then my armpits, then my abdomen. He also did the usual checking of blood pressure, eyes, heart rate, etc.

He found nothing to alarm him.

"I don't see any reason to do anything at this point. Let's just watch how the node behaves. If it gets too uncomfortable, we'll give you some chemotherapy. Right now it isn't called for."

I got dressed, and we returned to presidential politics, our general conversation. Canellos was a man of intense curiosities outside of medicine. He was interested in me and my family, in my experiences in government, in my travels around the world, in my political predictions. The lymph node was merely an opportunity for substantive conversation. This approach was deeply reassuring. No need to panic. No monsters in the closet tonight.

By 12:30 P.M. I was walking toward Faneuil Hall, where I was to meet my family and the Kails. Niki and Katina were strolling toward me.

"How was your meeting?" Niki asked obliquely.

"Fine. No need to do anything." Niki hugged me, and I picked up Katina and we both hugged her. No one around us seemed to recognize me, so the scene was not marred by a sense of being observed.

The day was cold and windy, but the pizza in Quincy Market was delicious, the doubledecker-bus ride interesting, and the state of mind just what the doctor ordered. Being with good friends like the Kails was delightful, because there was no need for pretense.

Two days later, Ray Shamie announced against me. He accused me of being a product of "big government, big business, and big disappointment."

I was being attacked as a candidate of big business, and I was the liberal Democrat and he was the millionaire conservative Republican businessman.

I called my Boston office and told them to get a copy of the press release and a tape of the announcement speech. We could use that quote when the campaign heated up. I had not been worried about mass defections from the business community, and Shamie's statement confirmed that I had been right not to worry. By that night, I had jotted down notes on five TV commercials that could feature that quote.

December meant more fundraisers and meetings with organizers and campaign workers. All during this time the various lymph nodes swelled and receded. A constant presence, but nothing too frightening.

I set aside two weeks on my schedule for the Christmas holidays. It would be the last break until the end of the campaign some eleven months later. It might have been regarded as a poor political decision, since it meant giving up several days of active campaigning. But I needed an interlude to refresh me and make the later campaigning sharper.

That was the theory. It was to make me eager to campaign.

I did spend three days in the office of Lowell city manager Joe Tully for a series of meetings with industrial developers, residential property owners, downtown property owners, and a second series on the issue of public education.

Those days were satisfying, because I really enjoy being a part of Lowell's recovery. But they were also very intense. I noticed in myself a different attitude toward the people we were meeting with.

I was impatient and intolerant. The owners of run-down rental properties were targets of my anger and scorn. The owners of downtown properties had to be pushed into considering rehabilitation investments, and I viewed their resistance as downright shortsighted, considering the financial incentives available.

These conferences made me sense the limits of my time and my concerns. I could not understand how an owner of deteriorating property could be unmindful of community attitudes. Is that how he wanted to be remembered? Where was his pride? It could not be explained on economic grounds, since the economics of Lowell had turned around and the properties could be sold at a handsome profit.

As the meetings progressed, I found myself growing ever more disgusted with the scarcity of larger vision. It all came to a head in our session on public education.

In mid-1983 I had initiated an effort to renovate Lowell's public schools, beginning with a review of the system by three outstanding consultants. The idea was vigorously opposed by the school-department establishment, including the superintendent and some members of the school committee. One committeeman had even accused me of being a draft dodger and of using techniques similar to those of Nazi Germany and Stalinist Russia.

Not your average civilized debate, but I was adamant about pursuing reform, not least because my children were to enter the system in September.

The meeting in Tully's office centered around a committeeman who was the key to our hopes for change. The November election had produced three new members, all in favor of change, and this incumbent would make a reform majority.

He had been a friend since high school days and had driven Niki around extensively during the 1978 campaign. He was also a friend of the superintendent's.

The meeting was called to secure a commitment to the consultants' study. He gave that commitment. But the discussion got around to the ultimate question—the viability of the superintendent. Neither I nor the city manager felt that the superintendent could, or would, institute serious reform. The situation would have to be faced. Our view was shared by the business community, the Lowell *Sun,* and most members of the parents' organization.

The committeeman resisted the direction in which the conversation was headed. His friendship with the superintendent was deep-rooted. He'd worked hard to implement the study, but he vigorously defended the superintendent and some of the personnel and management practices.

I exploded, accusing him of putting his friendship for the superintendent above his duty to his office, of personally jeopardizing the future of thousands of schoolchildren, and of other atrocities.

My vehemence surprised me and everyone else. My outburst was counterproductive. Old friends do not take kindly to tongue-lashings administered in front of other people.

That night I reflected upon what had happened. I realized that the lymphoma had given me a sense of urgency. I had come to realize that a person's stay on earth was truly temporary. Before, while I knew it was temporary, I felt it was infinite. There would always be time to do something. But now I had spent three months thinking about and negotiating with the reality that we are all going to die. We all had a date, and on the next day the sun would still be shining somewhere, the rain would still be falling somewhere, and the moon and stars would still be in their places. The earth was timeless, not those who inhabited it. What had to be done had to be done now.

I also realized that the lymphoma had given me a sense of legacy. What will they say when you're gone? Whether one lived one more day or forty more years, the question would always be there.

How could these property owners get through the day sanely if they had any concern about legacy?

"I see where Harry died yesterday."

"Yeah, just as well. The guy wasn't much for the city, the way he let his buildings go to hell."

"I suppose. But he made money at it."

"A lot of good it does him now."

I felt the same way about the school committeeman. He was a decent man, and he would support the study, but he would disagree on the critical vote of bringing in a new superintendent to clean house. He could decide whether there would be a transition, and he would affect the future of later generations.

Was I being fair or paranoid? You can't go through life telling people they should spend each day worrying about what will be said at their funeral. Or can you? This question and these feelings would reverberate through my mind as the days wore on.

Finally, Christmas came. It was a joyous time, made all the more joyous for me because I was constantly with Niki and the children.

Niki's parents are traditionalists about holidays, and so is Niki. Christmas is a major production, with gingerbread houses, wreaths all over, everything done to make it as wondrous as possible for the children. Christmas 1983 was no exception—and it was delightful.

Two weeks with the family—an uninterrupted two weeks. Dinner together every night, no rushing for airports, no "I'll see you in two days," no schedule.

Time for the simple byplay of family life, time spent in the company of those who care for you most, time for the rarity of everydayness.

It was an oasis, and I had to drink deeply at it in order to endure the next ten months of the campaign. And for those two weeks, I did drink deeply. It was a rare period, and I was refreshed by it.

At night we would put the children to bed after baths, stories, and the usual hassle over too much Christmas candy and "Look how late it is."

The lymph nodes were doing their swelling and receding, and that added reality to the simple activities.

I thought about how many of these moments I had forgone on my climb to political success and how many I would forgo as I continued that climb.

After the children were in bed, Niki and I would talk about the pleasure of being together like this. We had experienced the power and the glory, the excitement and the glamour of national politics. Washington did, indeed, throb, and we were in the midst of it all.

But in the next rooms, asleep, were what gave us true joy. And we had each other.

On Monday, January 2, the holiday was over, and we drove to Washington. The nine-hour trip was like all nine-hour trips with three children, a dog, and two cats stashed away amid the luggage—songs, games, arguments, hamburgers, naps, and frequent stops for the bathroom.

We arrived around 9:30 that night, and all hands tumbled into bed, leaving the luggage in the front hall for later dispersal.

The next morning I said goodbye and headed for National Airport and my return to Boston. I had three full days of mostly campaign but also some Senate activities. The campaign was to begin in earnest, and it was time to shift into full gear.

My two months of normal scheduling had quieted the rumors in Massachusetts about any illness. In Washington a story about leukemia had come to our attention. Someone in a Senate office knew someone who knew someone at Bethesda. Word was that Tsongas had leukemia. Chris Naylor was asked about it by the first someone, and Chris asked Dennis.

"Paul doesn't have leukemia," he said honestly.

She repeated that to the interrogator, and the denial plus the fact that I was behaving normally seemed to eliminate this speculation.

Tuesday night I returned to Lowell after a very full day. The house was cold, and I immediately went to bed in order to get warm. The cold sheets were a shock, and I lay there thinking how different a house feels when your family's not there. Two nights before, it had been full of life and exuberance and companionship. Now it was cold and empty and lonesome.

Well, I thought, I'm spoiled by those two weeks at Christmas. I'll soon get used to the old routine.

The next day was spent in campaign meetings and organizing sessions. We had begun a direct-mail operation and had found it very lucrative. It was generating thousands of new contributors who would serve as a web of support. This technique was new for me and had its aspects of Big Brother technology. But that is the modern age, and I had to be good at it.

The other parts of fundraising—meetings with large contributors and the normal fundraising events—were not going well at all. We had put together a finance council to straighten it out, and the first meeting had gone smoothly. We had lost a lot of time, but now there were people who could carry the load.

I returned to Lowell feeling good about the campaign. The finance council would shore up the major weakness, the organization was solid, there was no Democratic challenge in sight, and Ray Shamie was not getting much public attention.

Again the house was cold and empty, and again it depressed me. Once more into the cold sheets and once more a feeling of isolation.

When I left early the next morning I kept the thermostat turned up. Saving money on our gas bill was not worth the discomfort. I could look forward to a warm house when I returned that night.

The day was long and arduous, but not unlike other such days. I had been too busy to call home, but since I was going to be there the next day I thought Niki and the kids would understand.

That night the house was warm and comfortable.

But I wasn't. Rather than jumping straight into bed, I stayed up looking out the window at the darkened yard. Our Lowell house is gracious in a turn-of-the-century sense, and the yard is large and friendly. It was meant for a family to enjoy, and for six years it had been empty most of the time. In June the family would be here permanently, and so would the clamor and activity. The house would be happy.

But I would be in Washington at least three nights a week. We would rent our Cleveland Park house, and I would live in my uncle's house. He worked in New York during the week, so my using it would not inconvenience him.

I thought about six and a half years of driving to his house at night and going to bed surrounded by silence, while Niki was in Lowell trying to keep the family and law school in balance.

The prospect was gloomy. The cancer had exposed my need for Niki and the children, and the Christmas holidays had made me intensely aware of the preciousness of time spent with them.

Maybe if I flew back to Lowell on Wedensday nights and returned to Washington Thursday morning that would break up the separation. I would have to try it, because three or four nights away at a stretch was too much. This week had underlined the impact of separation. Perhaps I would get used to it. Perhaps the Christmas time together had heightened my expectations and they would have to be adjusted back down.

I fell into bed, and the sheets were warm. But I slept hardly at all.

On Friday I flew back to Washington and went straight to the office to take care of the accumulated paperwork. I couldn't stand it. By 3:00 I was at school waiting for Ashley and Katina to be dismissed from class.

"Hi, Katina!"

"Daddy, Daddy! What are you doing here?"

"I just thought I'd pick you up."

"Can Lizzie come over to play?"

"Sure."

We waited for Ashley.

"Hi, Dad."

"Hi, Ashley."

"I didn't know you were home."

"I just got here."

"Is Lizzie going to come home with us?"

"Yes."

"Well, can I have a friend over, too?"

"Sure."

It felt great walking into the house. Home, sweet home. How corny. How true. Niki had weathered the three days' separation better than I, but not by much.

We ate dinner at Armand's Pizzeria.

At 8:30 Niki went upstairs to put Molly to bed. Molly gave me a hug and a peck of a kiss, and grabbed her "baggie" (security blanket).

At 9:00, Ashley, Katina, and I went up as well. They changed into pajamas—"Did you brush your teeth?"—and climbed into bed. I read Katina one of her storybooks, turned out the light, and lay there with her. She talked for a while about little things and soon fell asleep. In the darkness I listened to her breathing and enjoyed the sense of serenity. After a while, I slowly took my arm out from under her, put the blankets around her, and left.

Ashley was reading in bed. I lay next to her while she finished the chapter. When she was done, I turned off the light and she nestled into my arms. Outside the window I could see the red light on top of the National Cathedral and remembered the first time she had spotted it and how excited she was about being able to see something like that from her bed.

We talked about what had happened in school during my absence.

Niki came in to kiss her good night and to say that she was tired and was going to bed as well. The downstairs had been secured for the night and the house was dark.

I lay there as Ashley fell asleep. And I thought about the three nights before in Lowell. I thought hard about it.

I began to realize how unworkable it all was. Here in this house with these people I was happy. Here was where I received my fulfillment and my emotional nourishment.

The idea of six and a half years of constant separation depressed me. Returning home late on Wednesday night only to leave early on Thursday morning would be no solution.

Staying in Washington was no better. Niki had a year invested in law school at Boston University; it would not necessarily be transferable. And we couldn't afford to stay here now that the Senate had put a limit on honoraria. It would require selling the Lowell house, and that would cut us off from a place we loved deeply. Besides, we wanted to go home, and Massachusetts was home. It was time for the children, and for us, to be surrounded by family and community. There was also a harsher reality. If the lymphoma ever became aggressive and overcame me, it would be too devastating for the family to lose me and move at the same time. And move where? The Lowell house would have been sold. It would mean a new house in a strange neighborhood.

No, we could not stay in Washington. We had to move back.

But could I pursue a campaign and a second term like this? I thought about it from every possible angle, and I couldn't see anything ahead but unhappiness for me—and for Niki and Ashley and Katina and Molly. The pieces did not fit anymore, no matter which way I turned them. They simply did not fit.

I got up from the bed, tucked Ashley into the blankets, and walked into the bedroom, where Niki lay awake in the darkness.

I lay down on the bed staring up at the ceiling with my head in her lap.

"I think we're going to have to think about not running again."

"What did you say?"

"I said I'm not sure that running for reelection makes any sense for us."

"What brought all this on?"

"Nothing in particular. An accumulation of things. I just can't see how six more years after a hard campaign serves any real purpose."

"Look. It's been a long three days away. Let's get some sleep and in the morning it'll seem more workable."

"But it's not workable, and a night's sleep will not change that."

"You're really serious, aren't you?" she said.

"Yes, I am. What do you think?"

We talked at length. It was a discussion, but in a strange way the conclusion had been settled before we began. The two weeks of Christmas had set in motion a need for normal family life, and it had become our priority.

For three months since that day in Bethesda we had never mentioned the possibility of my not running again. Running for reelection was a given. Part of what was inevitable and necessary and expected. Niki was acutely aware of how absurd the separation would be, but had not said anything.

Now I was aware of it, too.

We had to leave the Senate, not just Washington. We had to go home in the truest sense of going home.

But leaving the Senate? I'm forty-two years old.

After two months on the campaign trail, I was already tired of the politics of my job. But the substance of it still held me in a firm grasp. The Senate was the best place to be in my profession. Leaving behind issues I cared about would be very hard. For fifteen years I had been an intense political animal—to the point of being one-dimensional. How do you turn that off?

Niki took the role of devil's advocate, arguing the reasons for running again. The campaign would not be difficult, and after the election we could slow the pace. What about running again and then resigning in two years if it did not work out? No, that wasn't possible. We could not campaign knowing in our minds that it was not for a full term—it would make the second term halfhearted and would infuriate our supporters and contributors.

"What will you do if you are not in the Senate?" she persisted. "What will keep your intellect stimulated? You love the Senate, and there won't be anything like it no matter what you do in Massachusetts."

"Well, I could teach and practice law and do other kinds of things."

"It won't be the same."

"I know."

"But what if you really miss it and regret your decision?"

On and on. She would argue for running, and I would argue for not running. Finally I said to her, "How would you feel if we left and went home and I was no longer in the Senate?"

She was silent for a moment and then said quietly, "I'd love it."

That was it.

That ended the discussion.

Fifteen years before, I had lain on a beach at Magens Bay in the Virgin Islands and had decided to be a politician. For the next fifteen years I was consumed by that decision. Six campaigns and six victories. The United States Senate at age thirty-seven. Visions of going higher.

And now it was over. A decision made by two people, this time, in a dark bedroom on Macomb Street right in the center of political power.

The discussion and decision took about half an hour. Just like that. Half an hour after fifteen years of hard work.

And now it was over.

The decision seemed so easy, so natural, so obvious, so right.

We felt the sense of peace and relief that comes from recognizing what has to be. It was a wonderful moment. And very strange. Here we were about to walk away from a job most people would give their right arm for. How odd to be lying there saying we're going to leave the Senate.

Also odd was the fact that the cancer had no serious part in the decision. It was briefly referred to, but it was irrelevant to the larger question of a family needing to find itself. What counted was Paul and Niki and Ashley and Katina and Molly. Everything else was secondary. The cancer had only caused me to understand what truly made me happy, and what truly counted.

We lay in the darkness without speaking for a while, absorbing this sea change in our lives. We had begun together. We had campaigned each time. And now we were ending it together.

So how does the partnership vote on the motion to leave the Senate?

The partnership votes aye.

Any further business to come before the partnership?

Yes. Send a letter to the country saying that the Senate won't be the same without us.

Hear, hear.

So the decision took hold. Soon, however, we had to think about the practical details.

Now, how does one go about not running for reelection?

I leaned over, picked up the phone, and called Dennis. It was late, but he had been a full participant in all of this and deserved to know.

"I know it's late. Did I wake you?"

"No."

"I've got to tell you something you're not going to like."

"You're not going to run."

"How the hell did you know?"

"I just knew, for some reason."

"Well, what do you think?"

"It's your decision. Something like this is too personal for other people to comment on. If it's right for you, it's right. That's all there is to it."

"Dennis, I'm not asking you for a homily. I want to know what you think."

"Why? Are you decided or are you trying to decide?"

"It's decided."

"Well, homily or not, my reaction is the same. It's just personal. It's not a policy issue or a political matter. Only you know what's right in the circumstance."

"Well, let me ask it this way. Do you think I'm being impulsive and making a mistake?"

"It depends on what your reasons are."

I explained the reasons.

"In that case," he said, "you have no real choice."

I wondered how differently he would have reacted before Zachary had been born. His son had changed Dennis, and now he could appreciate what I was going through.

We arranged to get together the next morning.

Dennis knew me very well and had established an office policy for my staff. Whenever I proposed some outlandish idea, they were not to argue against it but just say nothing. In time I would think more about it and drop it. If I persisted after time for reflection, then they were to argue with me.

Was this another example of that?

I hung up and turned to Niki and related the conversation. When I finished, we returned to the issue of transition.

"You know, if we go back, we'll spend more time worrying about and working in the Lowell school system, since Ashley and Katina will be enrolled there. What would you think if I were to run for the School Committee?"

"What would happen if you weren't elected?"

"What do you mean, not elected?"

"Paul, an hour ago you were working on a campaign for reelection to the United States Senate. Now you're talking about the Lowell School Committee. I'm glad no one's around to hear you. They'd put you away."

Chapter 6

Announcement

On Saturday, January 7, 1984, we were awakened by Katina, who had jumped onto the bed.

Molly woke up soon after and was brought in to make it a foursome. Ashley, as usual, would sleep longer than anyone else.

Niki interrupted the game playing and told them to go watch cartoons. Katina was surprised. Usually we postpone the TV as long as possible.

She bounded off the bed and took Molly in tow.

"Well," Niki asked, "have you changed your mind?"

"No. Have you?"

"No."

"How about some apple pancakes?"

"Only if you make the orange juice and set the table."

So much for substantive discussion on matters of national significance.

We later shut off the TV and gathered the children around us.

"I've got something to tell you," I said.

"What is it?" Ashley said.

"I'm not going to run again for the Senate."

"Why not, Daddy?"

"Because I want to spend more time with you and give us all a chance to be together. I'm just away too much."

"But Daddy," Ashley said, "we've gotten used to your being away."

My heart sank. That was not a response I'd expected. It would take time to get her accustomed to my not being away, and I was now determined to invest that time. Her response solidified the decision.

"Does that mean we won't be able to campaign for you?" Katina asked plaintively.

"Well, yes, I guess so."

"Oh, Daddy," she said, "I want to campaign with you. Ashley did it last time, and now I'll never have a chance."

"Well, you can march with me in the parades this year."

Rather than being overjoyed by the decision, they were disappointed. Good grief!

Dennis came over later that morning. His premonition had prepared him for my decision, and he was comfortable with it. But we had to confront the details of a retirement announcement.

"When are you going to announce it?"

"I haven't thought about it."

"What are you going to say?"

"I don't know. What do you think?"

"And what are you going to do about the week in California?"

With the confusion of these days I had completely forgotten that I was supposed to be on a plane Sunday headed for California and four days of speeches and fundraising. It would be a real disruption. I took my schedule out of my briefcase.

Leave Sunday from Dulles Airport at 9:40 A.M. with Alex Drapos (a Worcester lawyer/friend/concert promoter/fundraiser). Arrive Los Angeles, go to Long Beach to meet Greek leaders at functions aboard *Queen Mary* . . . fly to Palm Springs for a speech . . . other speeches, fundraisers, meetings to develop contacts for other fundraisers, etc., etc. I had never even looked at the schedule.

How could I raise money for my campaign after I had decided not to run? How could I fake it? And how would I explain it to supporters later, even if I could fake it? They would be furious —and rightly so. Should I postpone cashing the checks? They would get very suspicious. Could I tell the organizers what was happening? No, they would feel compelled to let people know, and the news would be out.

The only solution was to cancel everything but the two speeches that were not campaign-related, one to the Outdoor Advertisers Association and one to movie-industry executives. But how can you cancel Sunday events on the previous day from three thousand miles away? I called Chris Naylor and asked her to meet with us. It was going to be very messy.

We then realized that Alex was flying to Washington that afternoon and was going to stay at our house. Should we phone him and save him the trip? No, better that we do it face to face.

What about timing? Well, as we had discussed back in October, we would first tell the staffs and then announce. I would return from California late Thursday. Friday was out, since it meant coverage would come on Saturday. The next chance was Monday, and that was the Martin Luther King holiday. Tuesday it would have to be. Tuesday, January 17.

But that was ten days away. In the meantime, we would have to cancel scheduled direct-mail appeals for campaign contributions.

If California events were dropped now and Massachusetts campaign activity as well, the rumors would fly. Keeping it all contained for ten days would be impossible. It had to be done sooner.

But how? Return from California on Wednesday night—one day earlier. Tell the Washington staff early on Thursday, fly to Boston, tell the Boston staff by noon, and make an announcement

at 2:00 or 3:00 P.M. Line up phone calls with Tip O'Neill and Ted
Kennedy and Boston meetings with Governor Dukakis and
Speaker McGee.

"Now," Dennis said, "what are you going to say?"

"I'll just say that I want to spend more time with my family.
That is the truth and will have to suffice."

"It won't be enough."

"Why not?"

"Because you can't explain to people who've worked for you
and voted for you that halfway through a campaign you've
suddenly decided to spend more time with your family."

"Well, they'll have to understand."

"But they won't. You don't give up a Senate seat so cavalierly.
The obvious question would be, why now? The Senate schedule
has been difficult for five years. You've raised half a million
dollars. You're going to have to be more candid."

"I'm not going to talk about cancer. Since I'm leaving government, it's a private matter now," I replied. Niki agreed with my
feelings.

Getting into politics is supposed to be complicated, not getting
out of it. In the end we decided I would mention health concerns
but nothing more. Dennis argued for full disclosure, but I was
hesitant, and Niki was strongly opposed. We would stick to the
middle ground.

Chris arrived, and when she saw Niki and me and Dennis, she
knew something was up. Although the news shocked her, we set
about figuring how to cancel the California campaign events
while leaving the speech appearances intact.

Dennis wanted to drop the entire trip, but I said no. Niki and
I were going to see one sister, Deirdre, who was about to have
a baby, and another, Tauni, who was pregnant. More important,
we wanted to get away to think everything over before the news
became public.

We worked out a format on the pretense that we had to see

my in-laws in San Francisco, where Deirdre was living. A poor excuse for someone in the middle of a campaign, but it would have to do.

We then laid out the task of informing people of the decision not to run. We phoned my sisters Thaleia and Vicki, Rich Arenberg, and Toots and Bob. Everyone reacted the same way. A sense of relief, of no surprise, of pleasure at the happiness it would mean for the five of us.

Late that afternoon I drove to National Airport to pick up Alex Drapos. He came out of the terminal looking for Doug McGarrah, whom he expected to meet him.

"Hello, Alex."

"What are you doing here? I thought Doug was picking me up."

"Well, I'm doing it. Get your bags and I'll be out front in the car."

He retrieved his suitcases and got in the car, and I drove away from the airport.

"I don't understand why you're here. Is Doug all right?"

"Yes, he's fine. I want to do the honors."

"I'm flattered, but there's got to be more to it than that."

"There is."

"Well?"

"I've decided to cancel all the fundraising events in California."

"What? After all that work? You can't! We're going to raise a lot of money out there, and you know we need it. Besides, it's Saturday afternoon, and the first one is tomorrow. It's impossible to cancel this late."

"Chris is already doing it."

Alex stared at me. This was not normal behavior.

"All right, what's going on?"

"I've decided not to run again."

He was absolutely speechless.

"We decided last night, and I'm going to announce it on Thursday in Boston."

He said nothing but just looked at me as we drove along the George Washington Parkway.

"Can you tell me the reason?"

"Yes, of course. In October I found out I have cancer. It's serious, but not all that serious. But it's made me realize that I have to change my life. It's time to be with Niki and the kids and live in Massachusetts."

"So that's why you disappeared for a week in October. I should have known something was happening. Why didn't you tell me? You know I would have kept your confidence."

"I know. I'm sorry, but we just wanted to keep it to ourselves."

He was very much upset, more than anyone else had been. I tried to reassure him with the details of the lymphoma, but he was slow to calm down.

"Are you sure you want to quit the Senate?" he said finally.

"Yes, I'm sure."

"But what will you do?" And for the rest of the drive home he argued with me about the financial realities of being a sick former politician. Health insurance. Life insurance. Job prospects.

"Promise me you'll not announce anything. Leave the schedule for California alone and see how you feel about it all when we come back."

"Alex, the goddam decision has been made. You're not going to get me to change my mind."

"Maybe not. But I'm going to try."

We arrived home, and the discussion continued. This time, I had Niki as reinforcement. Then my uncle, Telli Sismanidis, showed up unexpectedly. Telli is an economist in his seventies, born in Greece, very elegant in the traditional European sense and the relative most unabashedly proud of my political success.

I told him the story, but it was not easy. His wife, my aunt, had died of cancer three years before. She had been a nutritionist, well educated, well traveled, intellectually vital. He had suffered through her illness. It was a true love story, and he cursed the disease.

Here he was, thirty years older than I, enjoying my political status more than I was—and here I was telling him I also had cancer and my political career was over.

I ached for him as well as for myself. I saw the effect of my intention on someone who cared for me both personally and politically. Our family decision would not be limited to our family.

Alex seized on the occasion to reintroduce his argument for a change in the decision, this time with Uncle Telli chiming in: "You can't leave. . . . You must stay. . . . We will beat this cancer. . . . You have important work to do."

I said it was no use, the decision had been made, and we would all have to live with it. Uncle Telli embraced me the way I felt my father would have, had he been alive. Alex gave in and expressed warm feelings. The room was electric with emotion, and Niki and I felt surrounded by affection. For the first time in weeks, I could feel my eyes well up. Not from fright or anger or bitterness or frustration, but from thankfulness. I was not damned, I was blessed, and I had better really appreciate it.

Alex was then dispatched to have dinner with Doug McGarrah and try to explain the cancellations of the events which Doug had set up. Given the fact that he had also organized the thrice-canceled Pittsfield event, the Springfield town meeting, and other fundraising sessions that had been dumped back in October, he was bound to be upset.

And, indeed, he was.

When Alex told him I had canceled the California fundraisers because I wanted to see my sister-in-law in San Francisco, he was furious. "Doesn't he want to be senator, for God's sake?"

So the machinery was in place and beginning to function—the machinery to dismantle a political career.

Twenty-four hours had passed, and the decision had stuck. The number of people aware of the decision had grown from two to more than a dozen. It was not our secret anymore. It was now community property.

About three o'clock or so I woke up in a total fright. I had been dreaming that I was wandering along the Beltway outside Washington trying to find the Raytheon plant that was located somewhere in those rolling hills. I was applying for a job after being turned down everywhere else. I had to find the plant to submit my résumé, but I was hopelessly lost. My cancer had rendered me unemployable, and my family was going to be destitute.

As I began to climb out of the deep trance, I felt I had to phone Dennis right away, to tell him I had changed my mind. I would stay in the Senate to protect my family. Call off the plans for retirement.

Fully awake, I was shaking. I never had nightmares, and this one was devastating. I slowly regained my senses and composure. I had certainly absorbed Alex's concern over my employability. Was he right? Would the cancer cause people to shun me?

I could not answer those questions. Eventually I fell asleep again and dreamed no more.

In the morning I told Niki about my nighttime adventure, and we both laughed. In the light of a new day, it seemed so ludicrous, but I would not forget the fears it produced.

Later that morning we went to church and had our post-service ice cream. While I watched the Redskins demolish the Rams, Niki headed for the airport to meet Mary Anne Bresnahan, who had worked in the Washington office before going back to Boston. She had become very close to our children and had agreed to take a couple of days off to baby-sit while we were in California. Returning from the airport, Niki told her the entire story.

The California sponsoring groups for my speeches had split the flight costs—each paying for one ticket first-class. Having lived two years in an Ethiopian village and traveled in the most inelegant modes imaginable, I admit that I enjoy the pampering of long-distance airline travel. We read the Sunday papers, ate everything that was offered, and relaxed. We were alone and leaving Washington behind. We hoped to gain perspective and see how the decision felt from a distance. In Los Angeles we changed planes for Palm Springs, and by midevening we arrived at that resort.

I was to give my speech the next morning, and we had breakfast beforehand with our hosts from the Outdoor Advertising Association. Questions about the upcoming campaign and offers to help organize fundraisers were gently deflected.

It was odd being there, knowing that in three days I would be in Boston announcing my retirement. I had the urge to take everyone aside and reveal my secret.

I gave my speech, and we checked out of the hotel. Before departure I left a note for Tip O'Neill, who was also speaking there but was on the golf course, telling him that I wanted to call him Thursday around noon.

Then it was off to San Francisco to see my sisters-in-law, Deidre, who was about to give birth, and Tauni.

The next day I returned to Los Angeles by myself to speak to a group of motion-picture executives gathered by Jack Valenti, the Washington representative of the industry. The luncheon took place at Twentieth Century–Fox. Valenti was his usual gracious self as he introduced me, and I spoke about the federal deficit, foreign policy, and other issues of concern to the movie industry.

During the question-and-answer session, I was suddenly swept up by a startling sense of what it was to be a lame duck. Here were twenty-five of the most powerful men in the movie industry listening intently to my views and analyses of foreign and national issues. That was not new. They listened because I knew more than they did about these matters, simply because that was my job.

But as I answered their questions, I realized there was a lot more to it than just knowledge. They were listening because my office commanded respect—and because they were aware of the power inherent in being a member of the Senate. Power, whether real or imagined, is respected.

In forty-eight hours I would be a lame duck. I looked out at these men and wondered whether they would have attended had they known what I was going to do on Thursday. Would my expertise alone have attracted them? Would they be reacting with such respect? Probably not. In forty-eight hours the power would be stripped away. There would be no future influence, no future relevance. No one would again wonder if my destiny included higher office. No matter how unlikely that possibility, it still exists for most members of the Senate.

This was my final speech as a United States senator in the truest sense of the term. How many talks had I given over the years? Who had kept count? And the one today would be the last as a politician with a future.

I tried to gauge my feelings about all this, and there weren't any to speak of. I felt like a distant observer, a disinterested analyst. It was a fascinating little drama, and I was watching it all unfold. I wasn't happy. I wasn't sad. I was only intrigued. I wanted to remember the moment.

After the luncheon, one of the guests offered to host a reception for me. Valenti was pleased—this could result in some significant fundraising. He pressed me about it—when would I like to come back? I put it off, but he suggested other fundraising possibilities.

"Look, Jack," I said, "I very much appreciate your efforts, but why don't we hold off on this discussion until later? Next week we can talk and it will all be more relevant."

Valenti looked right through me. He was an old pro in my business, and I think he sensed there was more to this than I was letting on. Senators running for reelection do not lightly dismiss opportunities for fundraising. Instead of putting off these overtures, I should have been taking names, pumping hands, and nailing down dates right then and there. My behavior was downright aberrational for a seasoned politician.

He let the matter rest. "We'll talk next week," he said, and left.

At the airport before flying to San Francisco I called Dennis in Washington. All was quiet. There were no rumors, no inquisitive reporters poking around. The arrangements for Boston had been made. Marsha knew everything, but no one else.

"How do you feel about all this?" Dennis asked.

"About the same."

"Any change in the decision?"

"No."

"Any doubts?"

"None to speak of."

"Well, it's on to Boston, then. We'll be ready when you get back."

Niki and I spent the night in Berkeley at Tauni's house. I did not sleep well. I woke early and went down to the living room to phone the office. Knowing that tomorrow was the announcement day put me on edge.

The only telephone message for me was from Arthur Robbins, the developer of the Hilton Hotel for downtown Lowell. The hotel was the key part of a $40 million complex for the city, and the project had been kept together by the city manager and me with baling wire and glue. At three junctures I had had to use my influence to resolve financing or policy dilemmas. The complex was critical to the city's future, and I thought all the obstacles had been overcome and construction should begin soon. Was there another problem? Would it again require my intervention? Would I have to postpone the announcement so as not to be a powerless lame duck?

"Hello, Arthur. Paul Tsongas here."

"Oh, Paul, where are you?"

"San Francisco. What's the matter? Is there a problem?"

"No problem. You had spoken to me earlier about having a sculpture as part of the hotel, and I wanted to know what kind you were referring to."

After a brief conversation about sculptures I hung up. Soon we were heading out of Berkeley to the airport.

Goodbyes having been said, we entered the terminal, checked in, and boarded the plane. I took out my yellow legal-size notepad to write out my statement of retirement. As I was staring out the window trying to decide how to begin, the stewardess tapped me on the shoulder.

"Are you Senator Tsongas?"

"Yes."

"There's a message for you to call your office. It's urgent. There's a phone in the boarding area, but hurry, because we have to push away in three minutes."

Now what?

I ran off the plane and back up the passageway to the telephone booth and called the office.

Marsha answered. "Let me put Dennis on."

"What's up?"

"Dennis should tell you."

Dennis picked up the phone. "David Nyhan of the *Globe* called. He says there's a rumor you're going to announce your resignation tomorrow at two o'clock."

"Dammit. How did he find out?"

"I have no idea. The rumors are apparently circulating in Lowell and in Boston, but not in Washington. What should I tell him?"

"Don't tell him anything. Just say that I'm on my way back and I'll call him when I get there."

I thought for a moment. I had never lied to the press all these years. Beyond the ethical considerations was the reality that lying to the media was just dumb politics. It destroyed your credibility, and a deceived reporter was likely to be an unfriendly reporter. But this was the end of my career, and I wanted to go out my way. I told Dennis to tell Nyhan that it wasn't true, and Dennis agreed very reluctantly. Things were unraveling. I needed to buy time. I was three thousand miles away and would be virtually incommunicado during the flight.

Niki asked what had happened, and I responded with a stream of obscenities cursing everyone who was close to me. The only ones who knew about the retirement were family members and a handful of close friends and key staff. I went through the list in my mind. Which one was the Judas? Which one had denied me the dignity of a graceful exit on my terms? I wanted to punch someone in the nose.

Niki was incredulous. "Work on your statement and stop trying to conduct a kangaroo court." I hadn't even thought about the fact that I had delayed the takeoff because of a matter that was urgent only to me.

After a while I calmed down and forced myself to put things in perspective. No matter what was happening in Boston, the essential fact was that I was going to announce my retirement tomorrow. Whether someone had found it impossible to keep the secret was essentially irrelevant. I would write my statement. (A voice deep inside agreed, as long as we could return to the punch-in-the-nose approach after the announcement.)

I composed the statement with Niki's advice. It referred to a health problem, but was not specific. Once it was completed, I felt much better.

As we walked through the Dulles terminal around 5:00 P.M. and out into the wintry weather, the public-address system blared out my name. I had a message at the United Airlines desk.

Niki took the baggage to the car while I looked for a telephone booth. I called the office and discovered bedlam.

"The word is out," Dennis said. The *Globe* had said it was

going with the story of my retirement unless I personally denied its validity. That was not possible, just not possible. Events were getting away from us. The story would break a day too early.

Our original plan had been to go home and then meet with the Washington staff the next morning.

But now we agreed that Niki and I should proceed directly to the Senate office and tell the staff immediately, before they heard it from the media. Dennis suggested that we fly to Boston that night to meet the staff before the news was in the morning papers. But that would mean not going home, not seeing the children before the announcement. Tomorrow would have to do.

When we walked into my Senate office, the staff was assembled. The tension was extreme, and I began to tell the story.

"Back in October you'll remember I canceled a week of events. The reason was that I was at Bethesda Naval Hospital being tested. I have a disease. . . . "

I could not continue; emotion overcame me.

After a moment to compose myself, I began to describe the past few weeks.

My decision to change my life would also alter their lives. I had made a decision for them without their consultation and acquiescence.

I was circumspect about the illness. I referred to it as chronic —nothing more. I acknowledged its seriousness but did not identify it.

Some of the staff began to weep quietly. We had come to the end of an exciting era—abruptly. There had been no time to prepare, no time to absorb.

It took about half an hour to go through the explanation, let the emotions flow, and then laugh together about the clarification of the events of October. "Oh, that's why you . . . " Doug McGarrah was particularly upset, and I kidded him about his comment—"Doesn't he want to be a senator?" I also chided Chris Chamberlin about my "hernia."

When it was over I felt totally drained and yet appreciative of their concern and affection. We always referred to the office environment as a family, and here was the evidence—tears flowing down the faces of men and women.

Dennis reiterated the need to tell the Boston staff. Niki agreed; the children would have to wait. Here I was getting out of this business because of my family, and my first decision was to short-change them because of other responsibilities. But the Boston staff had to hear it at first hand.

We rushed to the airport with our California luggage, Dennis, Carol, their baby, Rich, Marsha, Chris, and Mary Anne Bresnahan. In the airport I met two Massachusetts friends and found it difficult to concentrate on conversation with them.

The entire episode seemed interminable. The flight was delayed for almost two hours.

At Logan Airport, Lawry Payne told us that the staff had been waiting at the Parker House since ten o'clock. It was now almost midnight. Worse still, word of the meeting had leaked and the hotel was full of reporters and camera crews filming the staff just sitting there.

Good Lord—the Tsongas operation seemed to be a direct line to the newspapers and television and radio stations.

I clearly could not go to the Parker House. We decided to send Lawry there and announce that the meeting had been canceled because it was so late. The staff would then be told to reassemble at the campaign headquarters at the Park Plaza. They were not to leave en masse, lest some enterprising reporter figure out what was happening.

To my surprise, the strategy worked. Whether it was the late hour or the bitterly cold weather, for once the press was kept at bay. The staff gathered amid the boxes and bumper stickers and signs of a political headquarters. Some had been with me for a decade, others had joined the campaign operation only days before.

This time I kept my emotions in check until the end, when Kay Petruzziello, a staffer of ten years' standing and a friend before that, hugged me.

I knew I had to control my emotions the next day or the press conference would be a disaster. I promised myself that there would be no more tears.

Niki and I drove to Lowell in the campaign car and reached home close to 2:00 A.M. We drove into the circular driveway off Wyman Street behind the house. I took the luggage and we entered the enclosed porch. On Mansur Street, the actual front of the house, TV lights suddenly went on. The media had been camped out there awaiting our possible arrival.

We entered the house while the reporters tried to film us. I felt as if I had just been indicted. We were thirty miles from Boston at 2:00 A.M. in eight-degree weather, and they'd been here all this time.

We went upstairs in that cold house to the bedroom without turning on the lights. From the windows we could see across the front yard to the street, where several cars were parked with their engines running.

"This is ridiculous," Niki said.

"Look at the bright side," I responded. "They're probably freezing their asses off out there. Let's get to sleep. Tomorrow will be quite a day."

The doorbell rang, but we ignored it. The cold would soon drive away the reporters.

Surprisingly, we both slept very well.

The next morning the doorbell rang. It was Jim Burns, our neighbor, with the papers. We let him in, and in so doing caused car doors to open and reporters to come up to the entrance as well. After a while Jim left to get us some breakfast from McDonald's.

We read the *Globe* and the *Herald*. The story was all over the front pages—and it was still six hours before the press conference. So much for doing it my way.

Jim returned with the provisions, followed by a camera crew. Niki looked at me, unshaven, hair uncombed, and in a bathrobe, and told me to get away from the windows. If ever anyone looked sick and disabled, I did. She sent me to shave and get dressed.

Strange, I thought. I looked fine physically. At no point during these months could someone have spotted signs of physical problems. I seemed healthy and robust and eager for more politics.

Another neighbor, Dave Frawley, came over and said that the Lowell *Sun* reporters were parked on the Wyman Street side and wanted to interview me before the two o'clock press conference, because they had a noon deadline. Just then, Joe Tully called and said I should give the *Sun* an early interview, since it was the hometown paper. I agreed to do so at eleven o'clock and phoned Ken Wallace, the managing editor and a high school classmate, to tell him while Dave went outside to inform the reporters. Even though the interview would not happen for two and a half hours, they remained outside in the cold just in case.

At 11:00 A.M. I walked outside to tell the *Sun* reporter and photographer to come in. I had known Mike Pidgeon, the photographer, all my years in politics, and it was like old times. When I reached their car, there was a TV camera in my face. The stations were now covering both streets. I stopped and chatted for a few moments with the TV reporter. Despite my irritation, I respected his tenacity and enjoyed the embarrassment it was obviously causing him.

We reentered the house for the *Sun* interview. I knew the reporter, Terry Williams, and his questioning was direct yet respectful. Funny, I thought, how awkward these reporters felt about asking me questions. The *Globe* had speculated about a heart condition. I told Terry that my heart was in good shape; it was something else, and someday I might tell him about it. "As you can see, I'm fine," I said, and looking at me, he had to admit I looked very healthy.

When it was over, Mike Pidgeon said he was shocked by the news.

"I thought for sure that you'd be in the White House someday."

"Mike, everyone feels that way about his hometown senator. It comes with the territory."

We prepared to leave for Boston. I had a 1:00 appointment with Governor Mike Dukakis, and a 1:30 meeting with Speaker Tom McGee. Before I left I called Tip O'Neill and my Senate colleagues Ted Kennedy, John Glenn, Lloyd Bentsen, and Robert Byrd.

My conversation with all of them was the same—shock, concern, and bewilderment. All of them, that is, but Kennedy. After discussing my career for a bit and how he'd miss me, Ted talked about getting proper medical advice for my illness. He told how he had spoken with several doctors when his son Teddy had come down with cancer in his leg.

Without its being said, it became obvious he knew I had cancer. The entire discussion was based on that premise. But how did he know? (I would later find out that he had told other senators about it in December at a conference in Wyoming. The Bethesda staff had not kept the news to themselves.) Of all my conversations with Ted Kennedy over the years, this was the most human.

As we started out the door, the phone rang. It was Frank Phillips, a *Herald* reporter. Frank had covered me years ago when he was with the Lowell *Sun* and I was on the City Council. He and his wife, Jenny, were former Peace Corps volunteers, so we shared that common background. Over the years we often spent part of our summers with them on Nantucket. Despite his being a reporter, he was a close friend.

He asked about my health. Did I have a heart problem? No. That didn't surprise him, since we often ran together and he knew I was in good physical shape and had been for years.

"Well, then, what is it?"

"I can't tell you. Not yet, anyway."

"Is it serious?"

"Yes, it is."

"It's not cancer or anything like that, is it?"

"I can't answer that."

"You mean you can't say it's not cancer?"

"Frank, I can't talk about it."

His voice changed from aggressive reporter to concerned friend.

"Look, off the record, tell me it's not cancer."

"I wish I could."

The conversation went dead as two grown men who often tried to out-macho each other in tennis and sailing and swimming and running choked up.

Finally I was able to say, "Listen, you bastard, I'll talk to you later," and hung up.

We drove to Boston—Niki, Nick Rizzo, Steve Joncas, who was my former economic development director, and I. I tried to figure out how to control my emotions during the press conference. They were not caused by my leaving the Senate or by the cancer. I was reacting to the expressed reactions of other people. As an instinctive loner whose feelings are contained within the family, I had trouble dealing with this outpouring of sentiment by staff and friends and others. But I didn't want the press conference to turn into a funeral.

I decided to open with whatever banter came to my mind, then read the prepared statement and take questions. I knew I could be humorous during the opening and the question period. But the statement was very serious. I wasn't good at reading texts, especially this kind. How could I get through it? I decided on a simple technique. Whenever I felt emotional, I would force myself to think of my children, whom I hadn't seen in five days, and remember how they would be affected by the way the press conference went. If it turned into a wailing session, they might as well come back to Lowell in June wrapped in black crepe.

I was not in that kind of condition, and the press conference was the time to make that clear. Any show of emotion would be interpreted as evidence that I was at death's door. I could not let that happen.

At noon we arrived under the arch of the State House and were met by several staff members and police officers, who escorted us to an elevator that took us up to the governor's office.

One of the officers looked me in the eye and shook my hand and said, "We're with you." I began to realize that this was not just a personal story, it was now public property. The decision to leave would cause all kinds of secondary responses throughout the state.

Niki and I met with Mike Dukakis in his office. Also there were my sisters, my brother-in-law, and Kitty Dukakis. Mike and I shared the same ethnic background, the same kind of education, the same ideology, the same age group. In 1978 when he was running for reelection and I was going for the Senate, we did not work together—each fearing a reaction if two Greek-Americans ran simultaneously for such prominent offices. In recent years that rivalry had subsided, and we had a good office-to-office and person-to-person relationship.

In the course of the discussion around the large table in his office, he said there was a judgeship available in the Lowell District Court, and it was mine if I wanted it.

I had to smile. A few days earlier I had sent a letter endorsing a Lowell attorney, George Eliades, for that post.

"No, Mike, I appreciate your concern, but I'm not worried about what I'll do later."

We shook hands, and I went next door, where his makeup person worked on me for the TV cameras. Physical appearance can often be distorted when TV is the medium. I was determined not to let the recent lack of sleep be interpreted as illness to a viewing audience.

Then it was into Speaker Thomas McGee's office for a similar session. McGee and I had become good friends through Nick Rizzo, and McGee and I were like Rizzo and me—we were totally incompatible philosophically, but the personal chemistry worked just fine.

We walked down the corridors, followed by the cameras, past the crowds, and into Gardner Auditorium. The place was packed. Friends, campaign supporters, staff, State House politicos, curious onlookers, reporters.

Niki and I worked our way in as the audience broke into sustained applause. I shook hands with a couple of reporters— Peter Lucas of the *Herald,* telling him our planned trip to Russia was still on, and Loring Swaim of the Malden *Mercury,* who had lately been critical of me. I reached the bank of microphones and was surrounded by what seemed to be a dozen TV cameras, some of them doing live coverage.

As I stood there, the fear about how I would do was gone. The test had been my reaction to Swaim. There was no hostility, but almost a sense of grateful comradeship for his covering me all these years. The combative edge was no longer there.

This was going to be fun.

I felt the way I had before the movie-industry executives. Comfortable and analytical. This was a great moment; I should enjoy it.

And I did.

"I never thought when I started into public life that this many people would come out to hear my position on acid rain."

The opening banter went easily, and the audience enjoyed it. They laughed at the quips far beyond their merit. It wasn't the humor, it was relief that there would be no morbidity.

Then I read the prepared statement. It was what I wanted to say, but it felt wooden. When I got to the emotional parts, I thought of the kids, and my trick worked. I was glad when it was over, and I could begin answering the questions.

"Senator, what will you do in private life?"

"I'm considering a career in broadcasting . . . " And we all laughed. "Given the lamentable state of political analysis in the media, I think I could do well."

This was great. A lot of softball questions from sympathetic reporters. A fitting tribute to fifteen years of hard work and substantive concern on issues.

Then it came.

"Senator, what kind of illness do you have?"

Yes, of course, this was serious business. The question shattered the illusion that the matter of my health would evaporate with my new status as a lame duck. People had to be thinking about "it," whatever "it" was. What's wrong with you, Senator, why are you giving up the Senate? How sick are you? You must be very sick to do this.

For me, the shock of the cancer had been an October phenomenon. I had digested and discounted the matter in the three and a half months from the hernia to the press conference. I had been through the hell of discovery, the coming to grips with the details, the comfort of awareness. Medically, my head was in January, but everyone else's was back in October. I had made my journey; they had not even begun.

Chapter 7

Leaving

In political life you quickly learn to anticipate questions at press conferences. You must try to formulate in your mind answers to likely questions so that your responses are complete—and not find yourself three hours later saying, "I wish I had said . . . "

I knew the question of health would be raised, but I had really not thought out the responses.

I answered by saying that I had never tried to manage the news before, but would do so today. The story was a "political one, not a medical one." The details of my health might be revealed later "if anyone even cares about it."

After all the years of public disclosure and public limelight, I had accepted the reality that senators relinquish claims to privacy. I had also become aware that the "leukemia" story in Washington some weeks before had been started by Bethesda people who didn't really know what I had. That meant that the truth would soon be discovered once reporters were assigned to the task.

Yet inside of me there were two strong emotions. First, I felt that since I was leaving public life I could now reclaim my

privacy: "I'm quitting, so take your grubby hands off my life."
Second, I recoiled from the idea of being the "senator with
cancer." I was proud of my career and the issues I had labored
over. I wanted to be remembered for my stands on industrial
policy, human rights, neoliberalism, historic preservation, arms
control, and the like.

"Senator Tsongas? Isn't he the one that had cancer?"

Being pegged this way was also galling for someone who took
so much effort to remain physically fit and did not use tobacco
or alcohol or whatever.

"There's Senator Tsongas. He's the one who wrote the book
on the new Democratic philosophy. By the way, did you know
he ran the Boston Marathon last month?"

Now, that's the way to go out.

For me, it was not to be.

The medical question hung heavy in the air. And it would
always be there. I had to learn to accept that as part of the package
of my public life.

The press conference was over; I had contained my emotions,
I had been humorous, I had "performed," and the stories and
editorials and columns and private comments would be very
kind. But I knew this was not the end. The political story was
over, and now the medical story would emerge. That story
would not, and could not, be contained.

As Niki and I left the auditorium, people were crying and
hugging and backslapping and shoulder-grabbing. In the midst of
this avalanche, Frank Phillips caught me. "On this other thing,
I want to talk with you. Can you find the time?"

I thought a moment. "Okay, I'll see you back at my office at
three-thirty." The "other thing" would have to be faced.

Niki and I walked out of the State House and down the hill
to the federal building. It was cold, and normally I would have
worn a coat and been driven. But I wanted the cameras to record
the vigor and physical exuberance of the event.

At the office everyone was relieved about how well the press conference had gone. For better or worse, my good performance was their good performance.

But it wasn't long before 3:30 came and Frank Phillips was in the doorway. I sent everyone outside, and I began to talk in detail on the condition that it not be used without my permission. I still hoped to suppress the story, but if it came out, I wanted the truth, not wild speculation. I had trusted Frank all these years, and he'd never let me down. I knew he'd be straight and honest.

After the interview, Niki and I decided to return to Washington. We got on the plane feeling very good about what had happened. It was the right decision, and we had handled it with as much grace as we could.

The children had been staying with Jon and Kem Sawyer, friends whose two daughters are the same age as Katina and Molly. They had been told about the cancer a couple of weeks before and had honored our confidence despite the fact that Jon is a reporter for the St. Louis *Post-Dispatch*.

We drove to their house on Porter Street and greeted the children we had last seen five days before.

As I hugged Molly, Ashley ran up to me.

"Daddy, they're talking about you in school!"

"What do you mean?"

"They're saying you're sick. Mr. Freeman and all the kids said they were sorry about your being so sick."

Our hearts dropped. They had heard the news from outside after all. Damn. I picked her up and said, "Do I look sick?"

"No."

We bundled them up against the cold and took them to the car.

Niki began it. "Children, Daddy and I have something we want to tell you, and when we get home I want you to listen to us very carefully."

We engaged in small talk in the moments it took to drive to our house. Once inside we put Molly to bed and then sat down with Katina and Ashley and outlined the entire story. When Niki referred to the cancer, they reacted with great concern, but as she explained the details they began to feel less threatened.

Niki was laying it all out to a six- and a nine-year-old, and they were absorbing the words analytically. No societal prejudice or undue abhorrence. Daddy was not going to be treated right now. Someday he might have to be. And if he did, he might be sick for a while. The doctors were very good and very optimistic.

The discussion went as easily as we could have hoped. We felt tremendous guilt about their having heard from someone other than ourselves. But they never reacted to that.

When we finished, Ashley read the comics and Katina went for something to eat. When it comes to dealing with the children, I defer to Niki's judgment, and at times like that I'm glad I do.

I later carried them upstairs to bed to demonstrate my health.

As I put Ashley to bed, I explained that cancer was like a snake. There are all kinds of snakes. Some are little garden snakes that don't scare you and others are like cobras that are very, very dangerous. I had cancer, but the kind I had was like a garden snake, and we should be very thankful. The analogy made sense to her, and she seemed to accept it.

Katina never mentioned my illness when I put her to bed, and that concerned me. We did not want her to suppress it and internalize her fears. We wanted it to be seen in full daylight and not be restricted to shadows and nightmares.

In Katina's case, we needn't have worried. She went to her first-grade class the next day and proudly announced that her daddy had cancer, but it was all right. It was a garden-snake kind of cancer (Ashley had told her) and was not a real problem. If only adults had the same equilibrium.

Later that evening, Frank Phillips called. He wanted to confirm that if anyone else had the cancer story, I would release the interview I had given him. Dennis had just told me that the *Globe* and the Washington *Post* had the story.

"In that case, can it be released?" he asked.

I hesitated. Either way there were problems. To suppress it meant taking a chance that the *Globe* and the *Post* possessed misinformation. To release it was an affirmative act of becoming the senator with cancer.

"Why not? That's the deal we made."

The story was coming out. I breathed a deep sigh of resignation. We had no control of events anymore.

The next morning we were awakened by Frank Daly, my Massachusetts press secretary, who read me the front page of the *Globe*. "Tsongas Votes for Home and Family." It was a sensitive handling of the event. He had not read the *Herald* yet, but would call when he had.

"What about the stuff on the cancer?"

"Where?"

"In the *Globe*."

"There isn't any."

"What do you mean, there isn't any? Did you go through all of the paper?"

"Every page. There's absolutely nothing on cancer. In fact, Mike Barnicle did a piece saying people should leave you alone on whatever the health issue is."

"You're kidding."

I had released Frank Phillips to do his story because I thought the *Globe* had it as well. I ran downstairs to read the Washington *Post*. There was a good piece by David Broder, but not a word on the cancer.

So the story was out because I had let it out.

I told Niki, and she looked at me the way someone looks at three-day-old dead fish.

What happened? Why hadn't the *Globe* and *Post* used it?

Soon after, Thaleia called. She told Niki about the *Herald*. Niki asked me to pick up the phone.

"The *Herald* has a story on your having cancer," Thaleia reported. "Frank Phillips wrote it."

"Yes, I know. I gave the damn thing to him and released him to use it because I thought the *Globe* had it too."

"There's nothing in the *Globe* about it."

"I don't have to be reminded."

"Jason and Emily"—my nephew and niece—"got very upset about it when they saw the headline."

"What headline?"

"The headline in the *Herald.*"

"What does it say?"

"It says, 'Cancer Forces Tsongas Out.'"

"What?"

"Yes, big, bold letters covering the entire front page."

"Oh, my God."

"Yes, it's really awful. Jason asked me why a paper is allowed to do something like that."

"But the cancer didn't force me out. The decision had to do with the family and . . ."

"Try telling that to all the people reading that headline right this minute."

"Read me Frank's story."

She did, and it was fair and accurate. But the headline composed by others was outrageous. "Forced out." I would be seen as someone who was slinking away like some kind of whipped dog.

I turned on the hot water, got undressed, and settled into the bathtub to try to soothe myself. The headline was crushing. The cancer story was out, and even though the story was proper, the headline would make the lasting impression. Forced out. Cancer Forces Tsongas Out. How stupid. If the cancer had forced me out, I would have retired three months ago, not now. I would have retired before we met with Canellos, not after. All the medical advice I had received indicated that I could have completed a second term.

I was overwhelmed with a sense of being victimized by the

Herald and, I had to admit, by myself. Suddenly I bolted out of the tub, got dressed, and called Niki upstairs.

Between expletives deleted, I managed to convey my decision to get the story out completely.

"Well, at this point, you don't have much choice," she said, "but try to be a little more successful this time."

I called Tom Winship, the editor of the *Globe,* whom I had known since I entered the Congress. We had met infrequently, but there seemed to be a mutual respect. I thought I could trust him.

He was on another line, and in a few minutes phoned me back. I told him how upset I was at the *Herald* headline. He said that they had had the same story but had decided not to go with it. So my information had been correct. How could I have assumed they'd sit on it?

"Look, Tom, I know this is unorthodox and I know it sounds like I'm trying to manage your newspaper, but I'd like to make a proposal."

"Go ahead."

"The cancer story is true. The story in the *Herald* is accurate because I gave it to Frank Phillips. The headline, however, is completely misleading. I cannot have people in Massachusetts thinking I was forced out. I am not being forced out. The story is much more complicated than that, and the whole point of why I'm leaving is going to be lost."

"So what are you proposing?"

"I want to sit down with your people and lay it all out in detail, and I'll try to arrange for you to interview Dr. Canellos, who's seeing me. I'll ask him to tell you everything."

"When do you want to do this?"

"I'll fly up there right away."

"Fine. I'll arrange it."

"It's not that simple. I want the interview to be made available to the TV stations and embargoed by them until Sunday morning."

"What do you mean, 'made available'?"

"They will film the interview and use it on Sunday."

He paused.

"Let me talk this over with my people. It's quite unusual. I'll call you back very soon."

I hung up with my heart pounding. I felt as if I were fighting back. No more being the victim. I was "hot news" for a few more days, and the coverage would be extensive. It had to be now. Next week would be too late. Niki had been there during the call. She was pleased that I was doing something to repair the damage.

In ten minutes Winship called back and agreed to the arrangement. He had one concern, however. If every TV station filmed the interview and one broke the embargo out of fears that someone else was about to, everything would collapse.

We then decided that one station would do the filming and then distribute it early Sunday to the others.

The interview was set for 2:00 P.M. at the *Globe*.

I then called Dr. Canellos, who readily agreed to participate. He was furious at the *Herald* headline and was delighted to help out.

Now, which TV channel? I had reasonably close contacts at all the stations, but I decided on Dave Mugar, the young entrepreneur who had taken over Channel 7. He was strongly community-minded, and I had come to know him when I was working for a new sports arena for Boston. I had confidence in his discretion.

I called him, and he also readily agreed.

I got dressed in my most official-looking black pinstripe suit in order to look senatorial, and a yellow tie in order to look cheerful. Impressions would be everything on television.

The plane ride seemed endless. In Boston, Frank Daly drove me through the stormy weather down Morrissey Boulevard to the *Globe*. I read both the *Globe* and the *Herald* on the way. Aside from the *Herald* headline, the articles were just fine. I especially appreciated Mike Barnicle's; he had never liked me, but had been at the press conference and had written a marvelous article. It made me choke up a bit, and one look at Frank's face did not help. What was it about all this that made grown men bubble up? It wasn't hard to figure out. Mix in one part giving up the Senate and one part dread of cancer and it's tailor-made for poignancy.

The press conference was one of my best moments in public life. But my feelings of self-congratulation and gratefulness dissipated when I looked at the *Herald* headline again. Back to reality.

When we arrived at the *Globe,* a TV cameraman recorded my presence. The chase was not over. The reporter asked me to confirm the *Herald* story. I said I was at the *Globe* to discuss the details of the illness and that everyone would know about it Sunday, including his station.

Tom Winship asked me if I would object if the paper promoted the Sunday piece. It would be done with taste, he assured me, and I said I had no objection.

I was to be interviewed by Chris Black of the *Globe,* who had covered me as a county commissioner and congressman when she was with the Lowell *Sun;* Loretta McLaughlin, the *Globe*'s medical reporter; and Joe Day of Channel 7.

For one and a half hours I answered every question, pursued every nuance, and exhausted their interest and mine. It was a civilized, discreet, and yet probing interview. When it was over, the only question was what would they use.

After the interview, Marty Nolan, the *Globe* editorial-page editor, and I talked about the contest for "my" seat. It was an appropriate sequel to the chapter on cancer. It was time to move on. The king is dead, long live the king. I would become old news, and public attention would focus on the process of succession. There was something almost soothing about it—a sense of having gone past something and then looking back on it.

Frank and I drove back into downtown Boston for a talk I had to give to the Foreign Affairs Council. Walking toward the building, we were met by Chris Naylor and David Goldman.

"The press is all over the front entrance. All the TV stations, everyone. It's a madhouse. You have to go in the side entrance."

We slipped into the building and met the group, and I gave my speech. Outside on the sidewalk, the TV crews were trying to film through the windows. Goldman tried to pull the drapes, which resulted in yells of protest.

I spoke on El Salvador, arms control, and the Middle East. Foreign-policy issues were always my favorite, and I never tired of talking about them. The audience was what you'd expect a Foreign Affairs Council to be—educated, discreet, and substantive. No untoward questions on health care were forthcoming.

The talk and the subsequent question-and-answer session were well received. I was very interested in the substantive matters and not at all preoccupied with the "illness" issue. That was a good sign.

When it was over, I went out the front entrance. Sneaking away from the press would have seemed like admitting there was something to be ashamed of. Ironically, the reporters had all staked out the side entrance, and it took them a while to reassemble.

"Senator, will you confirm the *Herald* story?"

"You'll find out on Sunday."

"Do you have cancer?" a TV reporter shouted.

"I did the interview today, and you'll have it on Sunday."

"Do you have cancer?" he insisted.

"Just read the papers, and you'll learn all the details."

The *Herald* reporter asked if his paper was going to have access to the interview.

"As a matter of fact, no."

"Why not? Is it because of the headline?"

"Yes."

"Is it fair to punish our paper like that?"

"Fairness is a two-way street."

The TV reporter reclaimed center stage. In a loud, insistent voice, he demanded, "Do you have cancer?" It was his third try, and he was again shouting. I just stared at him. Most of the reporters were embarrassed, but he was a real vulture. I was about to respond with some properly vulgar remark, but was grabbed by Chris Naylor and we began to make our way to the car, every moment caught on film.

It was an unsettling event, and I was really angry. How enjoyable it would have been to say something truly obscene— to give vent to the disgust I felt. But eventually I would have regretted it.

While waiting for the plane at Logan, I called Niki to report on the day. She said that Frank Phillips had phoned to see whether I was angry at him. So I rang Frank to reassure him that his story had been very fair. Certainly I didn't blame him for the headline. It didn't matter. He was upset because I had given the *Globe* an exclusive. "You are being punitive," he said. "Give us a chance to do it right," he argued. Here I was calling him to reassure him and he was making *me* feel guilty. And he was succeeding. I respected Frank's sense of fairness, and he did have a point. But it was too late. I had done what I had for good reason, and the *Herald* would have to live with it.

When I got to Macomb Street late that night, Niki was waiting at the door.

"Well, how do you feel about it now?"

"Just fine. For better or worse, it's all out there."

I told her about my later conversation with Frank and my feelings of guilt. "You're hopeless," she replied, only half laughing.

Saturday morning, Kendall Wallace of the Lowell *Sun* phoned to say they were upset by the *Globe* exclusive. The *Sun* thought it was being penalized because of the *Herald* headline. Additionally, inasmuch as the *Globe* and *Sun* readership areas were mostly different, giving the story to the *Sun* would not particularly affect the *Globe*.

Much of Saturday was spent trying, unsuccessfully, to resolve that concern.

I awoke Sunday morning with the knowledge that all across Massachusetts and in other parts of New England people were reading the details of my cancer. Most of the people I would have to deal with in my future life were among them. What would they think?

The phone began to ring. Call after call. The article was all we could have legitimately hoped for. It put the issue in terms that reflected my perspective. I wanted people to see it as I saw it. The story went a long way to bring that about. In addition, Dr. Canellos's quotes were reassuring. "He's in a lot better shape than I am." The headline of this story was: "Tsongas has one of the mildest forms of lymphoma."

All the TV stations used excerpts from the interview during the day. That night Channel 7 ran a half-hour program without commercials on the interview. It was just quiet conversation, focused on a human being talking about a long, long journey.

The press conference, the Sunday *Globe* articles, and the TV interview ended for all practical purposes the question of being "forced out." Some people would still not understand, but most of those I cared about would. I could go back to Massachusetts and continue my life without wearing a scarlet letter. I also believed I had been helpful to other people with cancer. By going public, I had taken away some of the mystery and stigma. The mail I received from cancer victims made me certain I had taken the right course.

For Niki and me, it was liberating.

For three and a half months we had kept a secret and lived a kind of halfway life. We knew something of great importance, but those we dealt with did not. It had removed us from them artificially. Yet telling them had seemed to be a far worse alternative. It was wandering into a great unknown.

Now it had all come out, and come out as well as we could have hoped.

The following Saturday the Washington *Post* published a column by Ellen Goodman of the *Globe* entitled "Quality Time." She began by describing how she had seen me once on the plane from Washington to Boston. I had had Katina along, trying to use the trip as a way of spending time with her. Goodman's article talked about families and priorities and how difficult it was for professional people to balance their responsibilities. It was the best piece about why I had decided to retire. I was concerned about her reference to the possibility that I had eight years to live, but otherwise it went beyond the cancer to the emotions I had felt while on Ashley's and Katina's beds just ten days before.

That morning when I went to the farmers' market to buy cider and apple pie, neighbors told me how moved they were by the Goodman column.

"Is this the daughter she was referring to?"

"No, this is Ashley. Katina was the one on the plane."

But Niki and the children knew I wasn't a role model. I wondered if I was going to spend the rest of my life avoiding symbols and labels. Requests for interviews came in from around the country. But I didn't want to be falsely idealized, just accepted for what I am. I had come to know my own needs—and leading the list were Niki and Ashley and Katina and Molly. The presumption that the Senate was at the top of that list and that I had sacrificed it for the sake of the family was nonsense. I was responding to what made sense for *me*. Since I didn't have a lot of close friends, the family was where I fulfilled my human aspirations. The Senate had become an obstacle to that. As Niki told a reporter later on, "We are a self-contained unit." Or as an old friend, Arnold Zack, wrote to me in a letter, "No one on his deathbed ever said, 'I wish I had spent more time on my business.'"

I chose to leave because of my needs. For my values. For what truly mattered to me.

In the next two weeks, several events occurred. I went to the Martin Luther King breakfast in Boston and truly felt like a private citizen. I looked at Governor Dukakis and Mayor Ray Flynn and the other officeholders as public officials seen from a private perspective. I now needed them to serve me as a citizen. I experienced a surge of dependence. I would be needing them to carry on the issues I had pushed. I realized how removed would be my influence. I felt the affection one has when one observes a good public servant.

I moved through the first week of the Senate session with difficulty. It was not the same as in Massachusetts; I was regarded as a dying man during the days following the announcement. One senator urged me to stay in the Senate. He argued that I would be taken care of by our medical and life-insurance policies. To go out into the world without such safeguards was foolish.

I decided I couldn't go through a year with colleagues and staff and reporters viewing me with pity. Consequently, Niki and I agreed to sit for an interview with the Washington *Post*, which ran on February 1, and that put matters to rest there as well. After reading the article, I said to Niki, "You know, after ten years in this town, all that I will be remembered for is the fact that I loved my wife."

"And what's wrong with that?" she replied.

Then I began receiving inquiries about my future plans. By the time a month had passed, I was talking to several universities about teaching positions, had arranged to meet with several large Boston law firms, and had begun to establish a real estate development partnership in Lowell. I recalled all too vividly my earlier fears about being unemployable. The cancer was significant, but my mind and my experience were apparently valued nonetheless.

Financially, the future would be manageable. But I knew I would occasionally ache about being out of the Senate. I knew there would be times when an issue would arise, and I would want to call a press conference or give a speech or file a bill or convene a meeting, only to feel frustration at knowing that no one would give a damn.

I would soon be yesterday's newspaper. The power to influence events and issues would be gone. What I cared about would still be there, but my capacity to help mold policy would not. Not in the same way.

As time went on and people saw me day in and day out, the cancer issue faded. I was being regarded as in the old days—in terms of both support and criticism. The criticism was especially comforting. As one who had been outspoken on various issues, I was accustomed to being the object of outrage from certain quarters. It soon began to reemerge. Little things at first, then more pronounced. Finally, full status. "Senator, you couldn't be more wrong when you say that . . ." Eventually, I no longer cared whether everyone could get past the cancer roadblock. Most people could, and that was enough.

I also received an astonishing volume of mail from people across the country. The open expression of sentiment was unexpected. Old friends, old enemies, new friends, strangers—many wrote and committed to paper feelings and thoughts that came from deep within. Their fears and hopes and philosophies were hinted at in a line or two or detailed in page after page. It was as if I had peeled back a layer of societal distance and discovered a wellspring of emotion and humanity. I came to understand that such sentiments exist in everyone—it just takes a crisis to bring it out.

Much of the mail was from people who had, or have, cancer of one form or another. They have kept that fact guarded, not wanting anyone to know. My public discussion of my experience had caused them to take heart. The fact that an elected official had "admitted" he had cancer was liberating to many. Doctors would later tell me of patients who brought with them articles discussing my lymphoma. On the street people would approach me and say, "No one but my family knows this, but . . . " and detail their particular illness—in most cases cancer, but often other illnesses as well. Indeed, two weeks after the announcement I told Niki that I wondered if a day would pass in which no one would confess to me that he or she too had cancer. More surprising were those members of Congress who would tell me of their cancer or other chronic illness. I was not uniquely afflicted.

On January 27 I left the office early, since the Senate was not in session, and picked up Ashley and Katina at school. Watching them bound out of the schoolhouse doors amid the clamor and screaming of their classmates always gave me pleasure. We walked home chatting about who did what to whom during the day's classes.

I decided to go up Macomb Street to visit a neighbor, the television newsman Jim Lehrer, who was recovering from a recent heart attack and a heart bypass operation. We had met only occasionally, but the encounters had been friendly and comfortable. Since he had a nightly news program and I was in politics, we had maintained a certain distance.

I rang the doorbell and was ushered into the house by one of his daughters. We sat in his living room with the sun coming in from the southern exposure. He was forty-nine, I was forty-two. We were both successful in our respective careers, we had married well, we both had three daughters, and we had spent a good part of the last few months contemplating our mortality.

The parallels in our thought processes during those weeks were remarkable, notwithstanding the fact that our illnesses were totally different. It is impossible, apparently, in such a circumstance not to wax philosophical, not to be reflective. The success of the Washington Redskins, the rise of neighborhood property values, the latest political machination—all were in the bin of irrelevance.

Jim described being in the hospital as his heart attack came on, and I remembered the terrible first phone call from Dr. Veach. We are so fragile, and yet we live on the assumption of eternal invulnerability. "Could this be happening to me?" How often that thought had crossed my mind.

As Jim related the thoughts that had occupied his mind during his brush with mortality, I had to smile. Mine were almost exactly the same.

We went from discussion of the physical to discussion of the meaningful. One comment he made has reverberated in my head ever since. We were talking about the conflict between family and profession—and how many people we knew in politics and in the media who had willingly or unwillingly sacrificed time with their families in order to pursue their ambitions. We talked appreciatively about people like Roger Mudd who put family first on their list of priorities even if it posed some risk to their careers. Lehrer said that as he lay in the intensive-care unit, he thought about his values and how he had allocated his time between his family and his profession. Upon reflection he was pleased to conclude that his priorities and his allocation had been just about right.

What a marvelous comfort for a successful person to be able to say that. I told him of admissions to me by congressmen and senators of their overwhelming feelings of guilt and remorse about their children who had grown up without a father's presence or affection. What price their success? Was it worth it? To some it apparently was. To others, I think not.

We ambled on quietly, and I found myself deeply satisfied about our shared experience. It was as if his "problem" had unlocked a door into a new world—a fearful world, very fearful, but deeper and more meaningful. And since I both liked and respected Jim Lehrer, it made my place less lonesome.

After an hour and a half or so, he walked me to the front door. I laughed about the image of two invalids getting together like septuagenarians trying to pass the time.

I walked back down Macomb Street in the warm sunshine. It was almost February, and the sense of spring was around, even if prematurely.

I thought about Jim's comments on his priorities. Home life was what I wanted, and that's why I was leaving the Senate. In the long run, it was what counted.

Strange about the cancer.

It still scares me when the lymph nodes swell up here or there. I still feel the pain or discomfort every day, and I am never without some degree of fear.

But I had been through the hell of October, and I had survived. I would reach my forty-third birthday in three weeks. I would get to be forty-three after all, and I would get to experience the coming spring. And beyond this one there would be many others. How long I will live, I don't know. What I will die from someday, I don't know. My earlier concern about heart problems may prove to be more relevant in time. But that's not the point.

By the time I reached my house, I had decided that I could write about this experience. I knew that in the near future I could go back and read the notes I took during the dark days—notes I could not even consider reading before.

What had the cancer, the lymphoma, done to me?

If all of a sudden I had the power to change history and prevent that original cell from undergoing its aberrational mutation, would I do it? Of course.

But I say that with hesitation.

The illness made me face up to the fact that I will die someday. It made me think about wanting to look back without regret whenever that happened. It made me appreciate Niki's strengths as I had never quite done before. I am blessed with a marriage that provides meaning. I would now look at my wife and "see" her in a way one does not in the rush of everyday life.

The lymphoma caused me to realize the preciousness of the moments of a child's development. I would have spent too much time away from my daughters had I continued my career. The attention and the power would have been seductive, and I would have enjoyed the former and, I hope, would have used the latter for good purpose.

But I would not have helped Ashley on her science project or accompanied Katina on her Brownie weekend camping trip or had Molly fall asleep in my arms in the hammock.

Life is a search for balance. We all have to bring the scales back to center.

Finally, my illness has forced me to understand that I have true spiritual needs whether I am healthy or unhealthy. It's hard to write about this. But I find I must attend church services in order to renew and refresh my sense of a higher being. God was always there for me, but always in a more removed way. Now, the entire matter of belief is central to me and gives me a truer sense of direction. The road is a long one, and I intend to continue on it.

These changes, or more accurately reinforcements, are a precious gift. The cancer gave them to me. I treasure them, and I will curse myself if I ever begin to forget, if I ever take my present health for granted, if I ever let a day pass when I don't feel gratitude that it has been given to me.

All this has made me a better person. Ironically, it would have made me a better senator, but that doesn't really matter.

My bright political career now seems irrelevant. I am leaving the Senate more qualified than I have ever been, but others will take my place. As an ordinary citizen, I can partake fully of the joys and responsibilities of family and give thanks.

So far, I'm off to a good start.

I notice if the sky is blue now. I see that God has given us the flowers and the rivers and the sunshine. I realize that life is wondrous in its natural and human dimensions.

There is a darkness as well. Every morning I know the fragility of my health and I am aware of my mortality. Every day something hurts somewhere, so I never can forget. There are new fears and new hobgoblins to come to grips with.

But, in truth, my great worry is that I will lose my current sense of values and perspective as the nightmare of October 1983 fades from memory. If I'm not ill for a long time, will I go back to the mindset I had before the "hernia"?

I pray not. I want always to feel as I do now.

I am here. I am alive, and I will partake of God's blessings. I have learned that those blessings must be truly appreciated if they are to have meaning. Let me, dear Lord, spend my life filled with the capacity to see what is before me and to be fulfilled in that sight.

A NOTE ABOUT THE AUTHOR

Paul Tsongas is a native of Lowell, Massachusetts, and a graduate of Dartmouth College and Yale Law School. He worked for the Peace Corps in Ethiopia and the West Indies, and served as Lowell City Councillor and Middlesex County Commissioner. In 1974 he was elected to the U.S. House of Representatives, and in 1978 to the Senate. After January 1, 1985, he plans to practice law in Boston and teach at the Harvard Business School.

A NOTE ON THE TYPE

The text of this book was set in a digitized version of Bembo, a well-known Monotype face. Named for Pietro Bembo, the celebrated Renaissance writer and humanist scholar who was made a cardinal and served as secretary to Pope Leo X, the original cutting of Bembo was made by Francesco Griffo of Bologna only a few years after Columbus discovered America.

Sturdy, well-balanced, and finely proportioned, Bembo is a face of rare beauty, extremely legible in all of its sizes.

Composition, printing, and binding by The Haddon Craftsmen, Inc., Scranton, Pennsylvania. Typography and binding design by Albert Chiang.